500 Classroom Tips
Intermediate

Table of Contents

500 Classroom Tips
Intermediate

About This Book

Looking for creative ideas to get organized and add some fresh appeal to your classroom routines? We've got 500 of them just for you! Whether you're a first-year or seasoned teacher, this idea-packed resource is your guide to creating and maintaining a motivating and productive classroom. We've collected the best classroom-tested ideas from *The Mailbox*® magazine and conveniently organized them into one comprehensive package. Inside you'll quickly and easily find surefire suggestions on the timely topics you need most!

- Classroom Routines and Events
- Organization Tips
- Curriculum Ties and Lesson Helps
- Student Motivation and Work Management
- Communications

Managing Editor: Debra Liverman

Editorial Team: Becky S. Andrews, Kimberley Bruck, Karen P. Shelton, Diane Badden, Elizabeth H. Lindsay, Debra Liverman, Sherry McGregor, Karen A. Brudnak, Sarah Hamblet, Hope Rodgers, Dorothy C. McKinney

Production Team: Lisa K. Pitts, Pam Crane, Clevell Harris, Rebecca Saunders, Jennifer Tipton Bennett, Chris Curry, Theresa Lewis Goode, Ivy L. Koonce, Clint Moore, Greg D. Rieves, Barry Slate, Donna K. Teal, Tazmen Carlisle, Amy Kirtley-Hill, Kristy Parton, Debbie Shoffner, Cathy Edwards Simrell, Lynette Dickerson, Mark Rainey, Karen Brewer Grossman

www.themailbox.com

©2004 by THE EDUCATION CENTER, INC.
All rights reserved.
ISBN# 1-56234-598-2

Manufactured in the United States
10 9 8 7 6 5 4 3 2 1

Contents

Absences

Carryall Caddy

Need an efficient way to organize assignments for a student who will be absent for an extended period of time? Cover a six-pack soda bottle carton with construction paper and colorful stickers. Put each day's assignments in a different slot, or arrange the assignments by subjects as shown. What an easy way to keep track of all those papers!

Colleen Dabney
Williamsburg Christian Academy
Williamsburg, VA

Absent Students

To solve the problem of locating extra reproducibles for a student who has been absent, I simply ask the student what day(s) of the month he missed. I keep 31 folders in a box—one folder for each day of the month. I make a few extra copies of each reproducible and place them in the appropriate folder. Students who have been absent can quickly locate the folders that contain their make-up work.

Brenda Pendleton
Ann Whitney Elementary
Hamilton, TX

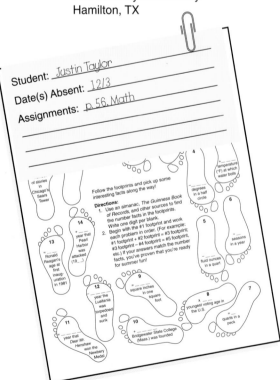

Keeping Tabs on Absent Students

Whenever a student is absent, I clip her reproducible assignments to an "absent work" form so that the student knows exactly what she's missed. If a lesson did not involve a reproducible, I have another student write the assignment on the space provided on the form. This keeps me from using up my limited supply of paper to run "a few extra" copies for each absent student.

Cynthia E. Britton
Longley Way School
Arcadia, CA

Assignment Center

Add function to your classroom walls with this timely tip. Decorate a large bulletin board to look like a calendar. Also make a seasonal header for each month. At the beginning of a new month, mount the appropriate header above the calendar. Then, before dismissal each afternoon, write that day's date and activities on an index card using different-colored pens: activities in black ink, notes in green, and assignments in red. Staple this card in the corresponding space on your calendar. Beside the display, place an assignment box containing folders labeled by subject. Fill the folders with corrected papers that were handed out while a student was away or work that an absent child needs to complete. After an absence, a student simply checks the assignment center and box to make up the work he missed.

Tamara Benning
Albany, OR

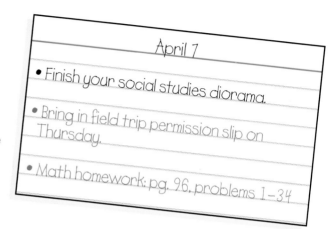

April 7

• Finish your social studies diorama.

• Bring in field trip permission slip on Thursday.

• Math homework: pg. 96, problems 1–34

Extra Skill Sheets

If you're tired of trying to track down extra reproducibles for an absent student, this timesaver is for you! In advance, make a few copies of a variety of reproducible skill sheets. Organize the sheets by skill in labeled file folders. Then store the folders in boxes by subject area. When a student who was absent needs a copy of a reproducible assignment, just pull a sheet on the same skill from your set of extras. Also use the extra reproducibles anytime a student needs additional practice on a specific skill.

Rosemary Linden—Gr. 4
Royal Valley Elementary
Topeka, KS

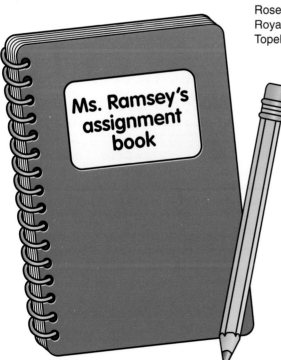

Ms. Ramsey's assignment book

Teacher's Assignment Book

If you spend valuable minutes each morning trying to gather makeup work for a student who's been absent, try this simple timesaver. Purchase a homework assignment book similar to those many schools furnish to students at the start of a new year. Each day, pencil in the assignments you give students. The next time a child asks about makeup work, simply direct her to your assignment book.

Brenda Ramsey
Foley Middle School
Berea, KY

Magnetic Morning Board

This attendance-taking technique is too good to pass up! Write each student's name on a sentence strip. Attach a piece of magnetic tape to the back of each strip. Then place all the name strips on a magnetic dry-erase board. Each morning have every student draw a small face to indicate his mood next to his name strip using a dry-erase marker as shown. Or vary the activity by having him sign in with a punctuation mark, a multiplication fact, or a spelling word.

Judy Wheeler—Gr. 5, Lincoln School
Schofield, WI

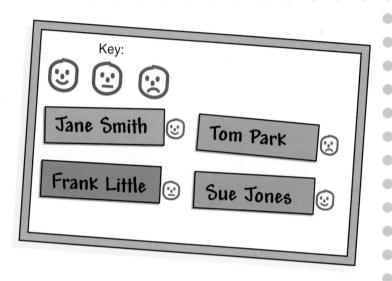

Key:

Jane Smith ☺   Tom Park ☹

Frank Little 😐   Sue Jones ☺

Monthly Planner

I use a large desk-size calendar as a blotter on my desk. In the calendar boxes, I record daily attendance, meeting times, parent phone calls, schedule changes, assemblies, and other information. When children bring parent notes for their absences, I cross their names off the calendar. This helpful technique eliminates having to wait until the end of a week, or even a month, to complete my attendance register.

Cathy Gallo—Gr. 5, Moriches Elementary
Moriches, NY

LUNCH COUNT

School Lunch   Lunch From Home

No-Fuss Lunch Count

Make taking the daily lunch count and attendance a picnic! Hot-glue two labeled wicker paper plate holders to a piece of decorated cardboard as shown. Next, attach pinch clothespins—each labeled with a different student's name—along the top of the board. Finally, title the board "Lunch Count" and attach it to a wall or bulletin board. As each student arrives at school, have him clip his clothespin to the appropriate plate. The clips that remain on the top of the board identify those students who are absent.

Brenda Fendley—Gr. 4, Blossom Elementary
Blossom, TX

Teacher Mail Basket

The most hectic time of the school day is when students first arrive. There's attendance to take. There are lunch forms to complete, coat zippers to unstick, and parent notes to read. To relieve some of the stress of this busy time, create a teacher mail basket. Students place any notes to the teacher inside the basket in the morning. Then, at the first available moment, you can check the basket for any mail. Morning confusion is lessened and your sanity is preserved for another day!

Michelle Kasmiske—Gr. 4, Monroe Elementary
Janesville, WI

Lunch Ticket Lifesaver

Has lunch become a hassle even before you've left for the cafeteria? Help is on the way! Construct a lunch-count board from poster board, library pockets, and paper clips. Mount a library pocket for each of your students on the poster board, labeling each pocket with a student's name. Put a paper clip on the front of each pocket. When students receive lunch tickets, have them write their names on their tickets and place them in their lunch pockets. In the morning, a student who wishes to order lunch places one of his tickets on the front of the pocket with the paper clip. The child in charge of the lunch count counts the tickets and sends the count to the office. Before lunch, tickets are distributed to their owners and lunch is under way, hassle-free!

Nancy Oglevie—Gr. 5, Sheridan Elementary
Sheboygan, WI

Permission Slip Relief

Are you sometimes swamped with returned permission slips or book orders? Free up your hands and your desk by pasting your class list to the outside of a large envelope. Laminate the envelope; then use a magnetic clip to hang it on the chalkboard. Tie one end of a length of yarn to the clip and the other end to a transparency marker. Now when a student comes to school with a permission slip, instruct her to put the signed slip in the envelope and use the marker to check off her name. You'll quickly be able to tell which child is missing a permission slip, and all the slips will be in one convenient place.

Diane Moser—Gr. 5, Sangre Ridge Elementary
Stillwater, OK

Three to Get Ready

Now that the kids are in your room, how do you calm them down quickly so you can all get to work? Prior to class, write three review questions on a transparency. As students enter the room, turn on the overhead projector to display the questions. Direct students to begin answering the questions in their journals as soon as they get settled. At the end of each six-week period, give each student who answered the questions and turns in a neat and well-organized journal an extra 100 percent test grade or other treat or privilege. In just one easy activity, you'll boost writing skills, review class material, and get students focused on the class period ahead.

Cyndi Harrell, Newbern Middle School
Valdosta, GA

> What is the difference between a common noun and a proper noun?
>
> What are the plural spellings of these words: child, bus, brush?
>
> What is the plural possessive spelling for the noun man?

Morning Made Easy

Easily take lunch count and attendance with a little help from your students. Place a laminated name card for each student in a pocket of a pocket chart. Behind the card, place a craft stick (see illustration). Hang the chart near your classroom door and place two plastic cups—one red and one blue—nearby. When a student arrives each morning, he turns over his name card; then he places his craft stick in the red cup if he is having hot lunch or in the blue cup if he brought his lunch from home. A student volunteer can easily scan the pocket chart to see the names of absent students and then count the number of hot lunch requests. What a timesaver!

Kim Smith, Meyers-Ganoung School
Tucson, AZ

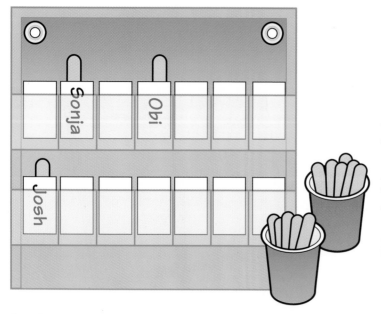

Class Elves

Here's an idea to help you begin each day smoothly. Have about three helpers, with their parents' permission, stay after school each afternoon. These students' responsibilities are to pass out seatwork and corrected papers for the next day. The next morning, the class will have something to do immediately upon arriving at school. Instructional time is also saved, and your day can begin efficiently. Our helpers are called "The Little Elves."

Mary Dinneen, Mountain View School
Bristol, CT

Coffee-Mug Timesaver

Use old coffee mugs and craft sticks to help with taking lunch and attendance counts. Write each student's name at the end of a different craft stick; then place the sticks in a mug labeled "Extras." Label additional mugs according to your school's lunch choices as shown. Every morning have each student place his stick in the appropriate cup. Just a quick check of the cups by you or a student helper, and your lunch and absentee counts are done!

Bonnie Gibson—Gr. 5, Kyrene Monte Vista School
Tempe, AZ

Please work on spelling worksheets.

What to Do

Need a way to quietly tell students what to do as they enter the room? Frame off a section of the chalkboard with laminated bulletin board border. Directions written in the space can be changed often without ruining the border, and students won't have to ask what to do.

Sharleen Berg—Grs. 4–6, St. Joseph's School
Redwing, MN

Munch Money

Save yourself the time and aggravation of dealing with forgotten lunch money by keeping a "Munch Money" jar in your classroom. At the beginning of the year, fill this jar with $10.00 to $15.00 in change. Allow students who have forgotten or lost their breakfast or lunch money to take out a loan from the jar. Since this is an honor system, students are responsible for paying back any money they've borrowed. As an end-of-the-year treat, use the leftover "Munch Money" to pay for an ice-cream-sundae extravaganza.

Phil Forsythe, Northeastern Elementary
Bellefontaine, OH

Birthdays

Birthday News Flashes

Honor your birthday kids each month with a display that recalls their first hours in the big ol' world. At the beginning of the year, ask each parent or guardian to complete a questionnaire like the one shown at right and return it to school with a baby photo of her child. Each month display the questionnaires of that month's birthday kids on a board titled "On the Day You Were Born." Your students will love seeing photos of their classmates and reading their vital first-day statistics!

Angela Newell—Gr. 4, Espirito Santo School
Fall River, MA

Name of child: Anna Elizabeth Cole
Date of birth: February 19, 1994
Time of birth: 6:18 A.M.
Weight at birth: 8 lb. 7 oz.
Length at birth: 20½ in.
Important news headlines on that day:
Triad Snowed Under
Special memories about that day: We had to get our neighbor, Mr. Jenkins, to drive us to the hospital in his four-wheel-drive vehicle.

Mark the Day!

Don't forget a single student's birthday with this handy tip. A few days before the start of a new month, ask each student celebrating a birthday that month to place a sticker in the appropriate box on your class calendar. Allow each summer birthday student to place her sticker on any day of a month of her choice. One quick glance at your calendar and you'll be ready to croon "Happy Birthday"!

Julie Granchelli—Gr. 4
Lockport, NY

Birthday Bottles

Bottle up your best birthday wishes with this cute-as-can-be idea. On the first day of school, have each student label an index card with her name, birthdate, and favorite candy bar (or a nutritious snack such as popcorn, raisins, or trail mix). Collect the cards. For each child, slit the back of a clean, clear plastic water bottle. Insert the child's treat through the opening; then fill the bottle with crinkled paper and confetti. Add a decorative postcard labeled "Happy Birthday!" as shown. Next, cover the slit in the back with a self-sticking nametag labeled with the child's name. Drop a birthday pencil through the bottle's top; then tie curling ribbon around the top. Before a child arrives at school on his birthday, place his special bottle on his desk. Celebrate weekend birthdays on the preceding Friday and summer birthdays on their corresponding days in September.

Peggy J. Kneen—Gr. 5, Fallen Timbers Middle School
Maumee, OH

Birthday Bash

Hold a private bash for your birthday kids with this easy-to-do monthly idea. Laminate and display a cutout of a birthday cake. Each month, use a wipe-off pen to label the cutout with the month and the names of students celebrating birthdays. At the end of the month, invite the birthday kids to a special birthday bash; then host a special lunch in the classroom, complete with ice-cream sundaes for dessert. Let students who have summer birthdays select a day during the last week of school for their birthday bash.

Cathy Ogg, Happy Valley Elementary
Elizabethton, TN

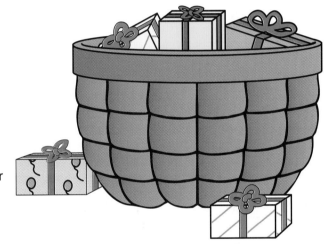

Class Birthday Basket

Make a student's birthday extra special with this gift idea. Program slips of paper with one-day class privileges, such as "Sit at any desk you wish" or "Choose your place in line." Gift wrap each slip inside a jewelry-size box. Then place the gifts in a basket. On a child's birthday, allow her to choose a gift from the basket. If her birthday falls on a weekend or during a school break, let her pick her gift the day before. For students with summer birthdays, have them choose their gifts during the last week of school.

Cathy Ogg
Elizabethton, TN

Once-a-Month Celebrations

If group birthday celebrations are more to your school's liking than individual ones, then this idea is for you! At the beginning of each month, create a schoolwide display showing photos of students who will celebrate birthdays during that month. If desired, include information contributed by the birthday kids themselves. Next, schedule a day on which parent volunteers can bring snacks for the birthday kids to enjoy at a special group gathering. If desired, distribute small treats such as pencils, erasers, or other school supplies. During the celebration, introduce each birthday child; then sing "Happy Birthday" together. Include children with July birthdays in the August (or September) celebration and those with June birthdays in the May festivities.

Gratsiela Sabangan—Grs. 4–6
Three Angels School, Wichita, KS

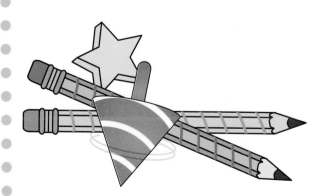

Birthdays

You're the Star!

Make each birthday child feel like a star with this bright idea! Obtain a class supply of berry baskets from a local grocery store. Place colorful shredded paper in the bottom of each basket. Then fill it with several items decorated with or shaped like stars, such as pencils, erasers, stickers, etc. Also include a package of Starburst fruit chews and a certificate granting the birthday child special privileges for the day. Before school on a student's birthday, place her basket on her desk. Observe summer birthdays by having each child choose a day during the year on which to celebrate.

Janie Rickman—Gr. 5
Oak Hill School, Lenoir, NC

Birthday Scavenger Hunt

Celebrate a student's birthday by sending him on a scavenger hunt for his favorite treat! On the first day of school, ask each child to label an index card with his name, birthdate, and favorite candy bar or gum. (Don't want to use candy? Then let students list a favorite class privilege instead.) On the student's birthday, send him on an errand. Hide his favorite treat in the classroom while he is gone. When the student returns, have the class sing "Happy Birthday." Then let the child hunt for his birthday treat as his classmates give hot-and-cold clap signals to direct him to the hiding place. Assign students who have summer birthdays "unbirthday" dates that are six months from their actual birthdates.

Mary D. Munoz, Dishman Elementary
Combes, TX

You Must Have Been a "Bootee-ful" Baby!

Acknowledge student birthdays a month at a time with this picture-perfect bulletin board. Duplicate the baby bootee pattern on page 33 onto light blue and pink construction paper. At the beginning of each month, write the name of each birthday student on an appropriate color of bootee (blue for boys, pink for girls). Have each birthday child cut out his bootee, attach a baby photo (or a recent one) of himself to it, and then decorate the cutout with pictures of his favorite things. Display the cutouts on a bulletin board backed with birthday gift wrap and titled "Happy Birthday to Our 'Bootee-ful' [month] Babies!"

Julia Alarie, Essex Middle School
Essex, VT

Shoebox Centers

To solve the problem of "But I don't have any space for centers!", I use shoebox centers in my classroom. Inside each individually labeled shoebox, I place directions for the activity, all the needed materials, and an answer key. A student can take a box back to her desk to complete or work in a quiet spot on the floor. When she has completed the center, the student writes her name on an index card and leaves the card sticking out of the box. This alerts me to check her work before I leave for the day. I write my comments and a grade (if desired) on her card; then I place the card on her desk for the student to read the next morning.

Wendy Shands
Lake City Middle School
Lake City, TN

The First 20 Minutes

My learning centers program is just the way to start the day! I divide my class into four groups. During the first 20 minutes of each morning, each student goes directly to one of four learning centers. Also during this 20-minute session, I meet with a remediation group of three or four students who work with me on any needed skills. Morning is a great time for centers because it helps students focus on the school day ahead.

Charlotte Hinson
Bellaire Elementary
Bossier, LA

Read ch. 6 in our novel.

Respond to ch. 6 in your journal.

Check math homework with a partner.

Complete a crossword puzzle.

Make a word search puzzle with spelling words.

Design a book report project.

Try to memorize the names of ten cities in our state.

Design a bumper sticker for National Pet Lovers Week.

Pocket Chart Centers

A pocket chart is just the tool to manage your classroom centers program. To begin, laminate a supply of red, yellow, and green paper strips. Each week program the strips with center activities as follows:
- Red strips: activities students must complete before the end of the day
- Yellow strips: extra credit activities students can work on after they've completed the red strip activities
- Green strips: fun activities that don't earn extra credit but still keep the brain in gear!

Place each strip in your pocket chart. Changing the strips is easy; just wipe the strips clean and reprogram them with new tasks.

Shannon Berry—Gr. 4
Heritage Christian School
Brookfield, WI

Centers

Center Choices

Intermediate kids love making choices, so I let my students choose the centers they want to work on. I label a magazine file for each subject. In each file, I place learning centers on that subject. These are centers that easily fit inside a large manila envelope or file folder. I place centers that are too large for the magazine files on shelves that are also labeled according to subject. When a student finishes his classwork, he is allowed to pick a center and take it back to his desk to complete.

Kate Luchtel—Grs. K–8 Tutor
Gardena, CA

Clever Clothespin Tip

To squeeze a little extra space for centers out of my classroom, I use an adhesive such as Qwik-Tac to attach pinch clothespins below or around my bulletin boards. I then clip file-folder games and other center activities to the clothespins. This simple trick makes my centers easily accessible—plus the colorful activities brighten up my classroom walls!

Jodie Sell
Wasola, MO

Center Organization

Track each student's use of classroom centers with this simple system. Divide your class into five heterogeneous groups. List the names of each group's members on a separate sheet of construction paper. Laminate each sheet; then back it with magnetic tape so that it will stick to the chalkboard. Write each center's title on a separate strip of construction paper, also laminated, backed with magnetic tape, and mounted on the chalkboard. At the end of each day, simply rotate the center titles to reassign the centers for the next day.

Adapted from an idea by Laine Scorti, Central Academy, Middletown, OH

Mary	Shyra	Stacey	Maggie	Sophie
Kirk	Neil	Meredith	Samuel	Derek
Kyle	Mohammed	Jackson	Beth	Maria
Megan	Kelly	Ben	Eva	Shane
WRITING	**CONFERENCE**	**READING**	**LISTENING**	**COMPUTERS**

Centers on a Table

If you've got a chart stand and a table in your classroom, then you've got a double-duty learning center! Place the chart stand in the middle of the table. On each side of the chart stand, hang a poster labeled with directions. Students can sit on either side of the chart stand and complete a center activity. Changing the centers is as simple as changing the posters!

Sharon Caskey—Gr. 4
Lincoln Elementary
Marshfield, WI

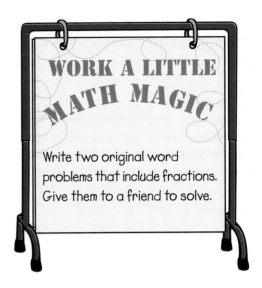

WORK A LITTLE MATH MAGIC

Write two original word problems that include fractions. Give them to a friend to solve.

Magnetic Centers

For fun centers your students will really stick with, look no farther than your metal file cabinet. Place a strip of magnetic tape on the back of a learning center; then stick the center on the side of your file cabinet. Or use appealing refrigerator magnets to adhere your center to the cabinet.

Jeri-Lyn Flowers
Cartersville Elementary
Cartersville, GA

A Two-Group System

Within our fourth-grade pod, we have a combined total of 17 computers. Each day students in my class spend 30 minutes working on these computers and 30 minutes in centers. To manage this hour, I divide my class into two groups: Group 1 and Group 2. Each of these groups is subdivided into four subgroups: 1A, 1B, 1C, 1D, and 2A, 2B, 2C, 2D. While Group 1 is working on the computers, Group 2 works on centers. I assign centers using a management chart (see the illustration). For example, if Suzy is in Group 2B, she will work on center 2 on Monday, center 1 on Tuesday, center 4 on Wednesday, and center 3 on Thursday. Once a student knows what her subgroup is, all she has to do is look at the chart to find her center assignment for the day. After 30 minutes are up, the groups switch.

Stephanie Speicher—Gr. 4
Elm Road School
Mishawaka, IN

	1	2	3	4
Monday	A	B	C	D
Tuesday	B	C	D	A
Wednesday	C	D	A	B
Thursday	D	A	B	C

Learning Center Tickets

Build accountability into your learning center program with this practical idea. Give each student a Learning Center Ticket, as shown, labeled with a number for each of your learning centers. Divide your class into groups—one per center. Rotate the groups through the centers at a pace that works best with your schedule (one center per day, all centers by the end of the week, etc.). When a student finishes his first center, he writes the center's name beside number 1 on his ticket; then he clips his work to the back of the ticket. As he progresses through the centers, he fills out his ticket and attaches his work. At the end of the day or week, collect work from one or two centers; then orally go over the remaining centers. Learning center tickets will increase student accountability and prevent casual attitudes about centers.

Clorinda Roache
Sherwood Park Elementary
Fayetteville, NC

Name: David

Learning Center Ticket

Center:	Name:
1. ✓	Grammar Getaway
2. ✓	Spelling Flash Cards
3. ✓	Geometry Game
4.	
5.	
6.	
7.	

This ticket is good for one admission to each learning station. Attach your work to this ticket when you complete it.

Bulletin Board Centers

Want to work with students needing extra help, but don't know what to do with the rest of the class? Turn your bulletin boards into activity centers that provide plenty of independent work for your more capable students. Post brainteasers, math challenges, writing ideas, or out-of-the-ordinary research topics on your bulletin boards. Direct students to head to the bulletin boards during those times when you need to work with small groups with no interruptions.

Lisa Groenendyk—Gr. 4
Pella Christian Grade School
Pella, IA

Simple Storage

Trying to find space for learning centers in an already-crowded classroom can be a real challenge. Make room for your learning centers with these space-saving ideas:

- Store learning centers in plastic milk crates placed on the floor along a wall.
- Purchase an inexpensive three-tiered rolling cart. Use it to hold file-folder activities and other learning center materials.
- Collect four same-size cardboard boxes. Use clear packing tape or glue to attach the boxes together as shown. Place the cross-shaped storage box on a desk; then fill each section with a learning center. By positioning a chair in front of each box, you've got four instant learning stations.

Deena Block—Gr. 4
George B. Fine Elementary
Pennsauken, NJ

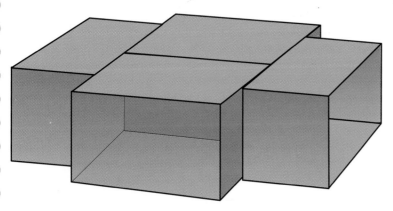

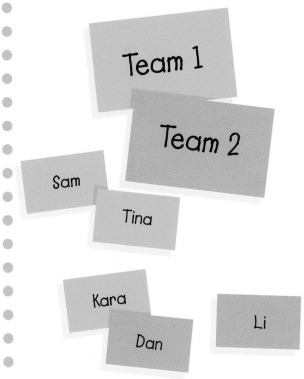

Learning Center System

Wondering how to flow 30 students through your learning centers without complete chaos? First, align five extra student desks along a wall. Label each desk with a different-colored index card: Team 1, Team 2, Team 3, Team 4, and Team 5. Place a center activity on each desk. Divide your class into five numbered teams; then write each student's name on a small index card that matches the color of his team's desk label. Stack each team's name cards (name side up) on a corner of its desk.

To move students through the centers, have each child whose card is on the top of his team's stack visit his team's center. When the student is done, have him put his name card at the bottom of the stack; then have him quietly inform the student whose card is now at the top of the deck to take his turn. At the end of the day, simply rotate the activities to different desks. By the end of the week, each team will have had a chance to complete each center.

Beverly Langland—Gr. 5
Trinity Christian Academy
Jacksonville, FL

Two Centers in One!

If you've got a classroom table, you've got two centers in one! I place all needed materials for my math or science center on top of a table. To make a second center without using additional space, I tape posters under the tabletop. Each poster is labeled with math problems to solve, story starters, or other tasks. Along a nearby wall, I've attached paper pockets to hold all of the necessary materials for completing the posters' tasks. My students love to recline under the table on mats and complete the activities.

Denise Mills—Gr. 4, Livingston Elementary, Covington, GA

Magic Wheel

Making sure that every student visits each of your learning centers doesn't have to be a management miracle! For a simple center assignment tool, cut two circles—one large, one small—from poster board; then laminate the circles. Fasten the circles together with a brad as shown; then divide them into sections according to the number of student groups. Use a wipe-off marker to label the outer sections with the names of your learning centers. Label the inner wheel's sections with your student groups. Post the wheel where it can easily be seen. When you're ready for groups to move to a different center, simply rotate the inner wheel in a clockwise direction. Continue rotating the wheel until it has returned to its original position. When you want to change centers or groups, just wipe the wheel clean and reprogram it.

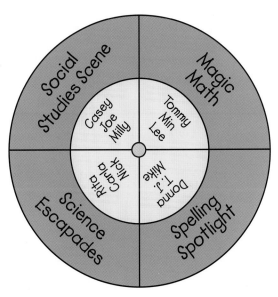

Merle Goess—Special Education Grs. 4–6
Albany Avenue Elementary
North Massapequa, NY

Class Jobs

The Job Squad

Every classroom can at times become cluttered, disorganized, and just plain trashed out! Create a classroom cleanup kit containing a feather duster, a whisk broom, cleaning rags, paper towels, glass cleaner, a sponge, dishwashing liquid, a pail for water, and disinfectant spray. Post a sign-up list for students that includes a job for everyone, such as erasing chalkboards, watering plants, emptying trash, dusting shelves, picking up paper, and alphabetizing encyclopedias. Then schedule a regular cleaning time in your classroom. Friday afternoons are ideal so that you can begin the week on the following Monday with a truly tidy classroom!

Penny Parchem—Grs. 4–8
Dallas, TX

Class Captain

Finding yourself frustrated by the everyday tasks that nibble away at precious planning time? Place a laminated checklist of daily jobs—such as taking attendance, erasing the board, and passing out school notices—in a binder. Each morning choose a student to be the day's class captain. Instruct the class captain to use a wipe-off marker to check off each job as he completes it throughout the day. The next morning wipe the checklist clean and choose another child to be the day's class captain. Now that's a timesaver worth saluting!

Paige Baker—Gr. 4, Barrington Elementary, Austin, TX

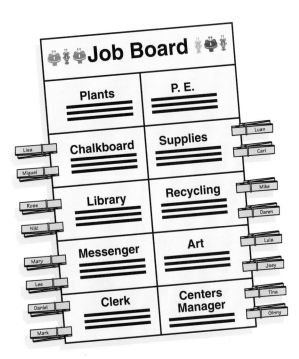

Student Job Board

Need a simple, easy-to-make display to help you keep track of classroom jobs? Divide a sheet of poster board into two columns; then divide the columns into sections equal to the number of classroom jobs. Write a job title and a brief description of it in each section. Laminate the poster board for durability. Next, write each student's name on both sides of a pinch clothespin. Assign two or three students to each job by clipping their clothespins in the appropriate section. Each week move the clothespins in a clockwise rotation to give students new jobs. Students can readily see the jobs they are assigned to and what the jobs entail.

Virginia H. Kotok—Gr. 4
St. Margaret School
Pittsburgh, PA

Whose Job Is It Anyway?

Assigning classroom jobs has never been easier than with this handy helpers display. Tack one large calendar for each classroom job on a bulletin board. Post the name of a different job above each calendar. Beneath each calendar staple a brief description of the job. Assign students to class jobs by writing a name (or names, depending on the job) in each school-day box on each calendar. That should stop all cries of "Whose job is it anyway?"

Andrea McMahan
Munford Middle School
Munford, TN

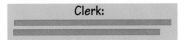

Clerk

S	M	T	W	TH	F	S
		1 Kathy	2 Steph	3 Beth	4 Greg	5
6	7 Labor Day	8 Liz	9 Sal	10 Jack	11 Mark	12
13	14 Matt	15 Dan	16 Cal	17 Zack	18 Lilly	19
20	21 Jill	22 Bob	23 Sally	24 Chris	25 Irv	26
27	28 Sue	29 Taj	30 Fred			

SEPTEMBER

Clerk:

Help Wanted

Billy

Jan   Amy

John   Dennis

Wanted: Class Helpers

Searching for a class helper chart that will really get the job done? Consider the position filled! Glue an employment page of an old newspaper to a sheet of poster board. Write each classroom job and its description on a different index card. Glue each card to a slightly larger piece of black paper; then glue each card to the poster as shown. Add the title "Help Wanted" and laminate the poster. Each week, assign jobs by using a wipe-off marker to write students' names on the cards. Wipe the cards clean at the end of the week so they can be reprogrammed with new names on Monday.

Yvonne Sturdivant
Guy-Perkins Elementary
Guy, AR

"Who-o-o's" in Charge?

Create this nifty classroom helper board and always know "who-o-o" has a particular responsibility. Make an owl from poster board for each student. Color the owls and label each one with a different student's name. Next, cut out and label a branch for each classroom job. Laminate the owls and branches for durability. Perch an owl on each branch on a bulletin board. Explain to students that the person whose owl is perched on a branch is the one who has that particular responsibility. Move the owls every two weeks so that each child gets a chance at doing a different job.

Donna DeRosa—Gr. 4
Good Shepherd Academy
Nutley, NJ

BETH
Line Leader

Class Jobs

Classroom Jobs Noted

Looking for a simple classroom job display? Write the name of each classroom job on a shaped notepad sheet. Laminate these sheets and post them in your classroom. Have each student write his name on a pinch clothespin. When you assign weekly jobs, have students attach their clothespins to the matching shapes.

Susan Rude
Harwood Elementary
Harwood, ND

Teacher's Assistant

Here's a great way to teach responsibility and give yourself a helping hand in the classroom. At the beginning of the year, select a different student each day to be the teacher's assistant. Give the assistant such tasks as taking attendance to the office, escorting ill or injured students to the clinic, returning library books to the media center, giving makeup spelling tests, collecting papers, and greeting visitors to the classroom. Allow the assistant to sit at your desk. After each student has had a chance to serve as assistant, use the position as a reward for responsible behavior. Since everyone has served as assistant and knows how much fun the job is, students work extra hard to earn the privilege.

Susan Keller—Gr. 5 Reading and Language Arts
Plumb Elementary
Clearwater, FL

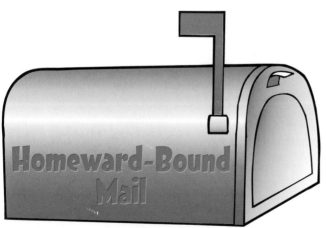

Homeward-Bound Mail

Recycle an old mailbox from home by giving it a new use at school. First, give the mailbox a fresh coat of paint. Assign one student to be the class mailperson for a week. When you receive notices that need to go home at the end of the day, immediately place them inside the mailbox and put the flag up. Explain to your mailperson that when the flag is up, he has notes to pass out to class members at the end of the day. No more will you find buried notes on your desk that should've gone home with students!

Michelle Kasmiske
Monroe Elementary
Janesville, WI

Computer Keyboard Covers

Looking for an inexpensive way to help your students practice memorizing the computer keyboard? Obtain the lid from a box of duplicating paper and cut away a flap from one of the long sides. Place the lid over the keyboard with the open side facing the student. Direct the student to place his hands inside the opening, under the box lid, and onto the keyboard. This allows the student to type without looking directly at the keyboard. Decorate the lid with Con-Tact paper for a more attractive cover.

Kelly Howell, Macedonia Elementary, Canton, GA

To Be Fair

How can you make the most of one computer when you have a classroom full of students? Post a list of student names near the computer. As soon as the first student on the list arrives for the day, she sets a timer for 15 minutes and works on the computer. When that student is done, she joins the rest of the class for the lesson in progress, and the next student on the list goes to the computer. Rather than make up any written work missed during computer time, the student turns in a piece of paper labeled with her name, the date, the name of the lesson, and "I worked at the computer today." With this system, you can be sure that everyone gets some computer time.

adapted from an idea by
Pam Williams—Gr. 4
Dixieland Elementary
Lakeland, FL

Taking Turns

With the help of a parent volunteer, two jars, and a supply of tongue depressors, my students get equal time on our class computer. First, I write each child's name on a separate tongue depressor and place these in a jar labeled "Waiting." The parent volunteer chooses two tongue depressors from the jar. When those two students' computer time is up, the volunteer places their depressors in another jar labeled "Done"; then she selects two more names from the "Waiting" jar. When all names have been chosen, the depressors are replaced in the "Waiting" jar and we start again. This system ensures that each student gets his turn and works with a different buddy every time!

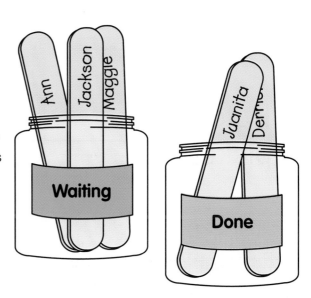

Maxine Pincott—Gr. 4
Oliver Ellsworth School
Windsor, CT

Computers

A Disk to Call My Own

Working between the computer lab and the classroom computer is a snap when each student has his own personal disk. Early in the year, have each student initialize and title a disk with his name. Whenever a student must stop midstream while working on a program in the computer lab, he has only to save his work to his disk. He can then take his disk back to the classroom and continue working on the classroom computer. This saves a lot of stress when computer lab time runs out before a student has completed a project.

Patricia Novak—Gr. 4
Meadowbrook School
Eatontown, NJ

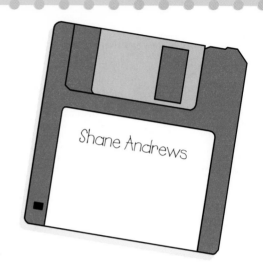

Shane Andrews

Computer Tutors

Maximize the use of your single classroom computer by utilizing peer tutors. At the beginning of the year, I instruct one student on the use of the computer. Then I schedule the rest of the class for peer-tutoring sessions. During study hall or computer class, the trained student instructs the next child listed on the schedule; then that student instructs the next child, and so on down the list. My class enjoys the reciprocal teaching, and I'm freed up to work with individual students.

Theresa J. Bowen
North Richland-Adams Elementary
Defiance, OH

Tongue Twister Keyboarding

Poor keyboarding skills seem to slow down most of our computer lessons. To motivate my students to become quicker and more accurate typists, I begin the year by having them type tongue twisters. Throughout the year, students warm up for computer class by typing tongue twisters. These humorous verses keep my students motivated while polishing their keyboarding skills.

Eileen J. Harford—Grs. 5–6
Orchard Middle School
Solon, OH

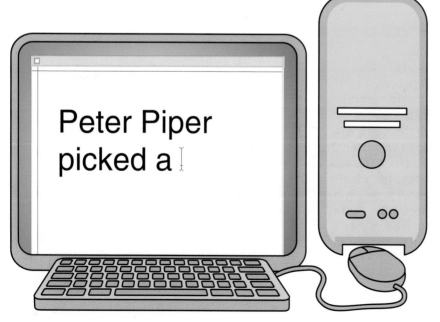

Peter Piper
picked a

Hanging Shoe Bag

Simplify diskette storage by using a hanging shoe bag. Label each pocket with the name of one of your software programs. Or provide storage for personal disks by labeling each pocket with a student's name.

Julie Eick Granchelli
Lockport, NY

Daily Computer Schedule

A daily computer-use schedule helps my class make the most of our one computer. Throughout the day, each student quietly dismisses herself from regular instruction at her scheduled computer time. While at the computer, she uses one of the two programs I have preselected to reinforce the skills of the week. A timer helps the student know when her 15 minutes is up. The student must make up any assignment she missed during computer time. This approach guarantees that each child gets one hour and 15 minutes of computer time each week. Students practice responsible work habits while improving their computer skills!

Lauri A. Shoup—Grs. 3–6 Math
Homer-Center Elementary
Homer City, PA

Computer Cups

Since I have 24 students and eight computers in my classroom, I assign three students to each computer. Each student is assigned a color: red, blue, or yellow. At each computer station, I stack three drink cups as shown. All of the "red" students work at the computers first while their classmates are completing seatwork or having individual instruction. When a red student finishes his computer assignment, he puts his cup on the bottom of the stack. Then it's the "blue" student's turn at that computer. After the blue student is finished, the "yellow" student takes his turn. I've found that this system works better if the faster workers are assigned as red students.

Brenda H. McGee—Gr. 4
Meadows Elementary School
Plano, TX

Computers

Computer Station Organizer

Want to eliminate the question, "Whose turn is it?" Organize your computer station with a three-ring binder filled with laminated construction paper cut to fit (one sheet per student). Open the binder so that it stands freely (similar to a chart stand). Use a wipe-off marker to write a student's name on each page. When a student is finished with the assigned computer tasks, he flips the page over to show the next person in turn. When all of the sheets have been used, simply flip the entire set back to the first sheet and repeat the process. Using wipe-off markers will enable you to reuse the notebook again and again.

Patti Derr—Gr. 5
Northwest Area Elementary
Reading, PA

Computer + Television

Tutor your entire class at the same time using one classroom computer and a television set. Most computers can be hooked up to a TV with a simple connector or a card that has been inserted into the computer. While one student runs the computer, you can teach new programs from the TV set.

Barbara Gerow—Gr. 5
Neil Armstrong Elementary
Port Charlotte, FL

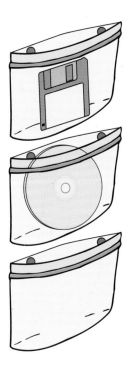

Saved by the Bag

Protect your floppy disks and CD-ROMS from accidental destruction or erasure by storing them in plastic zippered bags. Mount the bags on a wall near your computer. Any disks not in use belong in their appropriate bags. At a glance you can see if all the disks are put away. Students will soon learn that disks belong either in the computer or on the wall.

Caroline Johnson—Gr. 5
Citrus School
Upland, CA

Computer Lab Assistant

When using a multiloading program, send a responsible, trained student to the lab five minutes ahead of the class to boot up all the computers. This advanced preparation saves many precious moments of lab time.

Michele Miller Schaich—Gr. 4
Haw Creek School
Asheville, NC

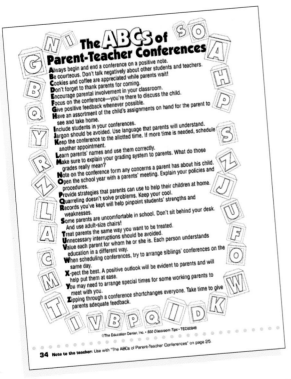

The ABCs of Parent-Teacher Conferences

How can you make sure that a parent-teacher conference is meaningful and helpful to all involved? Make a copy of page 34, and post it near your desk or slip it in your plan book. Take a few minutes to read over these conference basics before you meet with a parent. And be sure to make extra copies for beginning teachers and other coworkers.

Barb Witteman, Miami University
Oxford, OH

Plan Ahead!

I've found that planning for a conference is vital. Before a conference, I list three positive things about the student; jot down two subjects in which the student is doing well, plus his strengths in those areas; list questions I want to discuss with the parent; and note any plan that I can share with the parent to help with a particular problem area.

During the conference, I share these notes with the parent. I ask if she has any questions and if she would like her child to join us. If so, I invite the student's questions and comments. To conclude the conference, the parent, student, and I devise a plan for improvement. We also set a date to check on the progress of the plan.

Jean A. MacCoy—Gr. 5, St. Barnabas School
DeLand, FL

Students' Self-Evaluations

Try this icebreaker to get end-of-term conferences started on the right note. Each child in my class writes a self-evaluation of her accomplishments during the term, then lists behavior and academic goals for the upcoming term. She reads this composition to her parent at the beginning of the conference. This gives the child a chance to communicate with both her parent and me, plus proudly share her accomplishments. Students' self-evaluations are always right on target!

Nancy Murphy—Gr. 5, Converse School
Beloit, WI

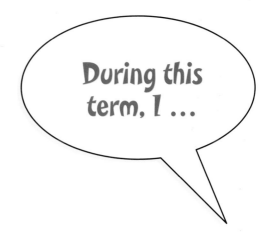

During this term, I ...

Self-Evaluation Letter

For open house, I have each student complete a self-evaluation report about her classroom progress. The report begins with a welcome from me, followed by a section for the student to complete (as shown), and then room for parent comments. As parents arrive, I give them their children's progress reports. Each parent reads the report, responds to his or her child, and then leaves the letter on the student's desk. Parents enjoy this part of the evening, and students love reading their parents' comments the next day in class.

Amy Schmitt Bissetta, Onondaga Hill Middle School
Syracuse, NY

- I am doing _____ in social studies class. The reason for this is _____.
- My teacher thinks that I am a pleasure to have in class because _____.
- So far, my grades _____.
- I am most proud of _____.
- I'm going to work harder on _____.
- To improve my grade, I need to _____.

Student-Led Conferences

Twice a year—once in October and again in February—our school hosts an open house. Before each meeting, I have each of my students organize his portfolio to share with parents; then I have him write an agenda for his "conference." In addition to sharing his portfolio, the student may wish to demonstrate the latest math skill on the chalkboard. Or he may wish to take his parents to the various centers in our room. My kids enjoy these student-led conferences and feel much more responsible for their own learning.

Teresa Williams—Grs. 4–5, Silver Creek School
Hope, British Columbia, Canada

Conference Notes

Conference Highlights for Parents

During a parent-teacher conference, so much is discussed that it's often difficult for a parent to remember everything once he leaves. During each of my conferences, I take lots of notes on bright notepaper. I include several positive comments about the student, suggestions for how the parent can help at home, and news about upcoming projects and due dates. The parent is able to talk freely, while I converse and take notes at the same time. At the end of the conference, I give my notes to the parent to keep as a home reference.

Karen L. Stephani—Grs. 5–6, Roosevelt School
Plover, WI

We Can Make THE Difference!

MARY PINECROFT

Call me if I can help:
555-5555 (School)
555-5545 (Voice Mail)

Business Card Swap

I designed a personal business card and then photocopied it onto pink and blue tagboard. During open house and conferences, I distribute these laminated cards to parents. I also ask parents for their business cards, which I keep in a file box. If it's more convenient for a parent, I'm able to contact him or her during the workday. Parents also have my number in case they need to reach me.

Maxine Pincott—Gr. 4, Oliver Ellsworth School
Windsor, CT

Parent's Guide

Conference minutes can pass by so quickly—and there's so much information to cover! To take better advantage of this precious time, I provide each parent with a copy of my "Parent's Guide to Mrs. Graf's Sixth Grade." This one-page outline explains my classroom policies and procedures. Parents really appreciate this guide and refer to it all year long.

Roseann Graf, Oak Ridge Elementary
Chino Hills, CA

The Week in Review

This organizational plan helps me prepare for conferences. Each week I store my students' checked papers in a large basket; then I distribute them on Friday afternoon. Students look over their papers, read my comments, and note their grades. Each child also receives his portfolio folder and a sheet titled "My Week in Review" (see the example). Each student chooses two papers that he wants to place in his portfolio and completes his week-in-review sheet; then he staples these three items together. I set guidelines for the types of papers (e.g., two from each subject) that I want students to choose. At conference time, I share the child's week-in-review sheets and accompanying assignments with the parent. If the student attends the conference, I invite him to share his papers with his parent.

Joan Fate—Gr. 4, Whittier Elementary
Clinton, IA

Name _____

Date _____

My Week in Review

1. This week I enjoyed _____

2. I think I have made progress with _____ because _____

3. I still need to work on _____

4. My behavior this week has been _____

5. My effort on my assignments this week has been _____

6. The book I am reading in my free time this week is _____

7. One goal I have for next week is _____

Response to This Week's Assignments

1. I chose assignment 1 because it shows that I can _____

2. I chose assignment 2 becasue it shows that I can _____

Parent Questionnaire

For a truly successful conference, plan for it! I always send home a parent questionnaire about two weeks before scheduled conferences. (See the reproducible on page 35.) I ask parents to respond to the questions so that I can better help them—and myself—prepare for our meeting. With this completed questionnaire as a guide, I can lead a much more organized conference!

Ann Nicklawske McGee—Gr. 4, Oakdale Elementary
Oakdale, MN

My Must List

For an effective conference, I always review my "must list":

1. Begin by saying something positive about the child.
2. Include the child in all or at least part of the conference. Ask for the child's suggestions.
3. Ask the parent what results he wants to see.
4. List actions that will be taken as a result of the conference.
5. Make a copy of the list for my files. Then give the list to the parent and child.
6. Suggest a follow-up call in two to four weeks to check progress.

Jane H. Reiser, Jones Lane Elementary
Darnestown, MD

Conference Postcards

When you want to ensure that a parent follows up on what was discussed during a conference, try this practical tip. Address a postcard to the parent as soon after the conference as possible. Thank the parent for participating in the meeting; then restate the role that you both agreed he or she would take in helping the child. End with another brief word of appreciation before dropping the postcard in the mail.

Shawn Parkhurst, Canadian Academy
Kobe, Japan

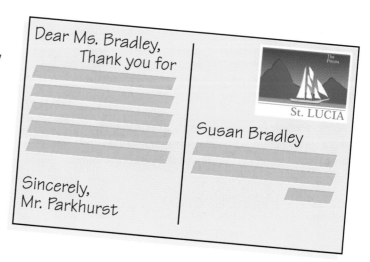

A Parent's Checklist

Most parents who attend conferences are prepared to listen to suggestions, but not to take notes. I've developed a parent checklist that includes areas in which the student needs improvement. It also includes suggestions on how the student can make those improvements a reality. Such items as "not completing homework" and "late assignments" are balanced with extra help suggestions. Every category may not be relevant to each child, but by the end of a conference, the checklist is individualized to a student's needs. A parent not only has a record of any problems, but also has strategies for solving them.

John Hagan Jr., Grafton Middle School
Grafton, MA

Parent-Teacher Conference Checklist

Student's name _____ Date _____

Areas that need improvement:	Suggestions for improvement:
☐ completing homework	☐ complete extra credit assignments
☐ completing work on time	☐ team up with a "study buddy"
☐ bringing materials to class	☐ complete a center activity
☐ participating in discussions	☐ complete a bonus project
☐ listening in class	☐ keep a class journal
☐ cooperating in groups	☐ keep an assignment calendar
☐ _____	☐ _____
☐ _____	☐ _____

Family-Teacher Conferences

About two weeks before conference day, each of my students takes home a notice that lists available time slots for appointments. When all of the notices have been returned, I send a confirmation letter to each parent. This letter includes the designated conference time, plus several encouraging comments about the child's progress. I ask the parent to respond by writing some positive statements about his child and his child's work. The student is also encouraged to add comments about his successes in school. In addition, I also ask that the parent and child cooperatively list any questions or concerns that they may have. When it's conference time, I encourage both the parent and child to attend—and to bring the letter. During the conference, we review the student's progress, discuss any questions and concerns, and write a brief plan of action for continued success. I later send a follow-up postcard thanking the parent for taking part in the conference.

Phil Forsythe, Northeastern Elementary
Bellefontaine, OH

While You're Waiting...

For conference day, I prepare lots of materials for parents to read while waiting for their appointments. These materials include learning activities for home, plus articles about learning disabilities, gifted programs, cooperative discipline, contracts, and other relevant topics. I also include several children's magazines and book order forms. Parents enjoy reading these items—plus it helps them pass the time while they're waiting.

Jeannette Freeman—Gr. 4
Baldwin School of Puerto Rico
Guaynabo, Puerto Rico

Events

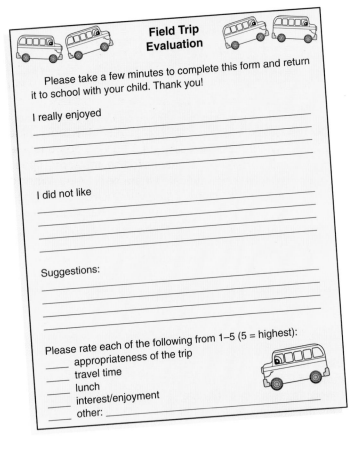

Field Trip Evaluation

Please take a few minutes to complete this form and return it to school with your child. Thank you!

I really enjoyed

I did not like

Suggestions:

Please rate each of the following from 1–5 (5 = highest):
_____ appropriateness of the trip
_____ travel time
_____ lunch
_____ interest/enjoyment
_____ other: _____

Field Trip Evaluation

After a field trip, I give each parent chaperone a brief form to complete like the one shown. I ask parents to share their opinions about the trip and what changes they would suggest. With this simple form, my students' parents know that their input matters to me.

Marianne Hanson
Lanham Christian School, Lanham, MD

Teacher Conference Tip

When I attend a conference or seminar, I take along a package of small index cards instead of a notebook. I write individual ideas from the sessions on separate cards. When I return home, I can easily file the cards in the proper subject folders so that they'll be handy to locate and use at a moment's notice.

Bernice Hagan, Memorial Middle School
Fitchburg, MA

Speaker's Presentation Planning Sheet

Have you scheduled a special speaker to visit your class? Then ensure a successful presentation by preparing the speaker and your students beforehand. Make a copy of the planning sheet on page 36. Sign your name where indicated; then fill out the blanks above the dotted line. Mail the form to the speaker a couple of weeks before the scheduled presentation. As stated on the form, the speaker will complete the form; then he or she will make a copy to send you. Use the information on the sheet to prepare your students and classroom for the speaker's visit. Because you've taken the time to prepare everyone in advance, the presentation will be more focused, successful, and meaningful.

Robert Rubenstein
Eugene, OR

Our special speaker today is Mr. Addison

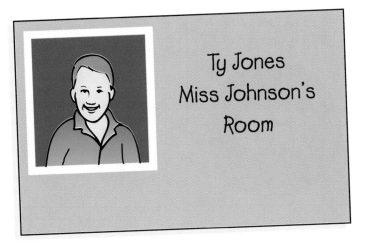

Ty Jones
Miss Johnson's
Room

Student ID Cards

Keep track of your students in a snap with this teacher-tested idea. Obtain a photo of each student; then glue the photo to an index card labeled with the student's name and your name. When a student leaves the room for any reason, have him place his identification card on a bulletin board labeled with different destinations (office, rest room, speech class, etc.) to indicate where he is going. When on a field trip, pin the student's card to his clothing or hand it to a chaperone so she can quickly identify the students for whom she's responsible.

Jaudon Marlette—Gr. 4, Arbor Ridge Elementary
Orlando, FL

Drink Passes

Patrol the path to the water fountain with this simple idea! Make drink passes titled "Morning," "Recess," and "Afternoon" from construction paper. Distribute a copy of each different pass to each student. Once he has used his three passes, a student's drink privileges are over for the day.

Patti Eby—Gr. 5, Shalom Christian Academy
Chambersburg, PA

Beanbag Markers

How can students leave the classroom to use rest rooms without interrupting you for permission? Use two different-colored beanbags: one assigned to the girls and the other to the boys. Place the beanbags somewhere in your classroom so that students can get to them without distracting anyone. When a student must be excused, he gets the correct beanbag and places it on his desk. Only one boy and one girl can be out of the classroom at the same time, and it only takes a quick glance to see who is missing.

Laura Reeb—Gr. 4, Anderson Mill Elementary
Austin, TX

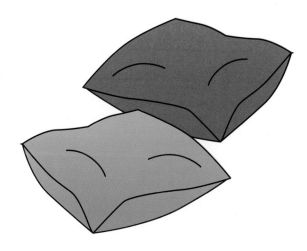

Class Movement

Rest Room Traffic Control

"May I go to the rest room?" can be a distracting question in the middle of a lesson. I've solved this problem by making two signs—one each for my boys and girls—with the words STOP and GO on opposite sides. Each laminated sign has a magnetic strip on each side so that I can attach it to the corner of a chalkboard. When a child needs to go to the rest room, he or she flips the correct sign to STOP. This lets the remaining boys or girls know that someone is out of the classroom and they must wait their turn. When that student returns to class, he flips the sign back to GO. If there are times during the day when I don't want anyone to leave the classroom (during a test or while I'm giving directions), I turn both signs to STOP.

Mary T. Spina—Gr. 4, Bee Meadow School
Whippany, NJ

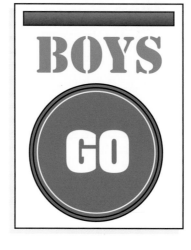
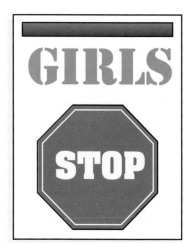

Student-Finder Chart

It's a challenge to remember all the different places in our school where my students may be. To help me out, I write all of my students' names down the left column of an incentive chart. In each blank across the top, I write a different place or job: rest room, office, errand, nurse, Chapter I, etc. I post the chart on a bulletin board near the door, along with a cup full of pushpins. When a student leaves the classroom, she places a pushpin in the appropriate column, letting me know her destination. The kids are great about remembering to use the chart, and I always know where everyone is!

Gina Morrison—Gr. 5, Bowie Elementary
Grand Prairie, TX

Punch Pass

Name_____

Date_____

Drinking Fountain   Library
1 2 3 4 5   1 2 3 4 5

Responsible Requests

Curb frequent requests to visit the drinking fountain or library with this idea. Each Monday give every student a pass as shown. When a child needs a drink or wants to visit the library, punch his pass. When all the numbers are punched on a student's punch pass or if he loses it, he must wait until the following week for a new one. Monitor the punch passes by copying them on different-colored paper each week.

Connie Ericson—Gr. 4, Mable Woolsey Elementary
Knoxville, IL

The ABCs of Parent-Teacher Conferences

Always begin and end a conference on a positive note.

Be courteous. Don't talk negatively about other students and teachers.

Cookies and coffee are appreciated while parents wait!

Don't forget to thank parents for coming.

Encourage parental involvement in your classroom.

Focus on the conference—you're there to discuss the child.

Give positive feedback whenever possible.

Have an assortment of the child's assignments on hand for the parent to see and take home.

Include students in your conferences.

Jargon should be avoided. Use language that parents will understand.

Keep the conference to the allotted time. If more time is needed, schedule another appointment.

Learn parents' names and use them correctly.

Make sure to explain your grading system to parents. What do those grades really mean?

Note on the conference form any concerns a parent has about his child.

Open the school year with a parents' meeting. Explain your policies and procedures.

Provide strategies that parents can use to help their children at home.

Quarreling doesn't solve problems. Keep your cool.

Records you've kept will help pinpoint students' strengths and weaknesses.

Some parents are uncomfortable in school. Don't sit behind your desk. And use adult-size chairs!

Treat parents the same way you want to be treated.

Unnecessary interruptions should be avoided.

Value each parent for whom he or she is. Each person understands education in a different way.

When scheduling conferences, try to arrange siblings' conferences on the same day.

X-pect the best. A positive outlook will be evident to parents and will help put them at ease.

You may need to arrange special times for some working parents to meet with you.

Zipping through a conference shortchanges everyone. Take time to give parents adequate feedback.

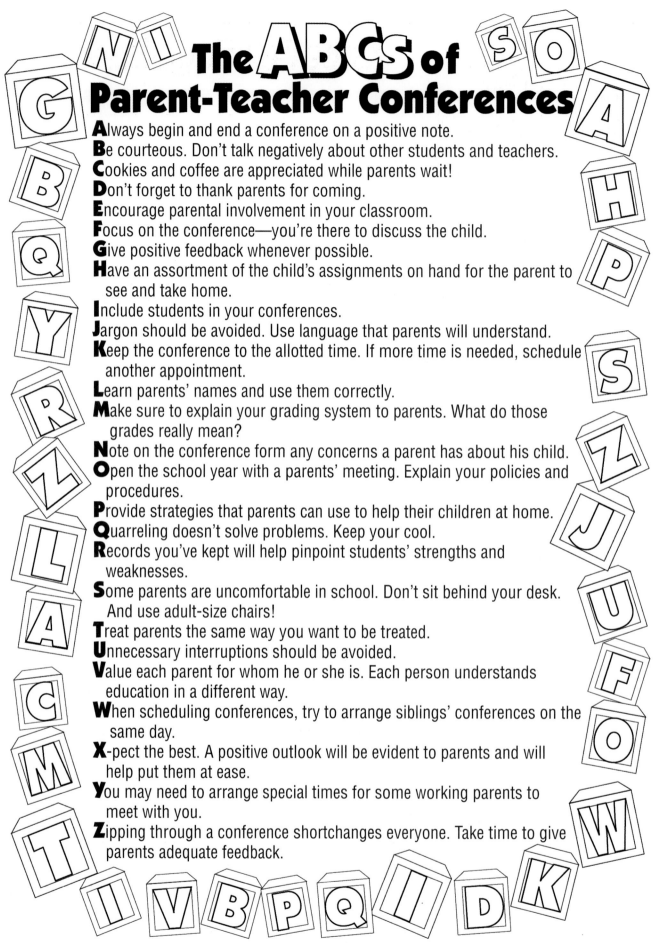

Let's Pull Together!

_____
date

Dear _____,

    Would you please take a few minutes to answer the questions below? Your responses will help us prepare for our upcoming conference. I look forward to meeting with you on _____

_____.

    Please return this questionnaire before our scheduled conference day.

                                Thank you,

- What subject(s) does your child enjoy most?_____
  Why?_____
  _____
  _____

- What subject(s) seems difficult for your child?_____
  Why?_____
  _____
  _____

- About how much time does your child spend each night with homework and reading?
  _____

- Does your child participate in any afterschool activities? _____
  If so, list them: _____
  _____

- Please list any concerns that you think we should address during our conference:
  _____
  _____
  _____
  _____
  _____

Note to the teacher: Use with "Parent Questionnaire" on page 28.

35

Date _____

Presentation Planning Sheet

    Our class is very excited about your upcoming visit. This sheet will help you prepare for your talk. I have already completed some of the information below. Please take a few minutes to fill in the rest of the sheet as indicated. Make a copy of this sheet for yourself; then send a copy to me so that we can adequately prepare for your visit.

Thank you,

_____

Speaker's name: _____

Speaker's address: _____

Speaker's phone number: _____ Date of presentation: _____

Location of presentation: _____

Contact person: _____ Phone: _____

Audience (number and age): _____

- -

Please fill out this information:

Topic (including any subtopics): _____
_____

Approximate length of presentation:*_____

    *The average attention span of a person younger than 14 is about ten minutes. The key to holding an audience's attention is to vary the way you speak and what you include in your talk, to include audience participation activities, and to use a variety of visuals such as posters, the overhead projector, demonstrations, etc. Try to include personal anecdotes and experiences, startling facts, quotes from famous people, poems, and humor relating to the topic in your presentation.

What should our class know about your topic before your visit? _____
_____
_____

Are there materials you would like duplicated beforehand to distribute to students? ___ If yes, please list the materials or attach a copy(s) to this sheet. _____
_____

How should seating be arranged? _____

Circle any equipment you will need:

microphone	chair	table	blackboard
overhead projector	podium	television	VCR
large pad of chart paper	slide projector	filmstrip projector	film projector

    other: _____

How would you like to be introduced? _____
_____

What should students know about you? _____
_____
_____

Would you like students to list their questions before your visit? _____

Would you like to review these questions before your visit? _____

Note to the teacher: Use with "Speaker's Presentation Planning Sheet" on page 30.

Contents

Class Library

Classroom Library Organizer

Keep your classroom library organized in a snap with this helpful tip. Use a marker to write the first letter of the author's last name on the top of each book as shown. Then shelve the books in order by author. One quick glance across the tops of the books identifies any misplaced volumes. Plus, students can reshelve books for you in no time.

Laura Eliason—Gr. 5, Woods Cross Elementary
Woods Cross, UT

Library Rescue!

Keeping track of all the books in your growing classroom library can be a daunting task! With the help of a database program, you'll get organized in no time. Create four alphabetically arranged categories on the database: title, author, code, and student name. Once the program is in place and all the books have been cataloged, have several capable students keep the catalog current. With this tool it's easy to add new books or locate those already in the library.

Antoinette Parry—Gr. 5, Wellwood International School
Baltimore, MD

Classroom Library Organization

Looking for an easy and practical way to organize your classroom library? I bought several inexpensive dishpans. Then I organized my books by either genre (mysteries, nonfiction, etc.), topic (animals, friendship, etc.), or author and placed each set of books in a different labeled dishpan. This simple system serves two purposes: My students can get to the books easily and are therefore more motivated to read. When students look for a particular type of book or one written by a specific author, they can easily find what they're looking for!

Michelle Zakula—Gr. 5, St. Roman School, Milwaukee, WI

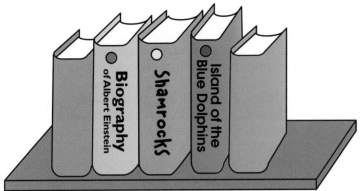

Color-Coding Trade Books

Is your classroom full of trade books that need organizing? Help your students find needed books more quickly by color-coding them with self-sticking, colored dots. For example, attach blue dots to the spines of all chapter books, red dots to short books, green dots to books about famous people, and yellow dots to informational books. You may want to reinforce the dots on the spines by covering them with pieces of clear tape.

Bo Miller—Gr. 5, Mapleton Elementary
Mt. Sterling, KY

Organizing Literature Titles

Instead of using a file box of notecards to organize book titles and genres, I've developed a more useful system for visual learners such as myself! I use a three-ring binder with dividers labeled by subject area and literary genre (mystery, biography, realistic fiction, etc.). I photocopy the front cover and either the back cover or summary page of each book that I may want to use for whole-group, small-group, or individual reading. If the book is in my classroom collection, I make the copies on white paper. I use blue paper for books from my personal collection and yellow paper if the book is in our school library. Within each section, book titles are alphabetized by author. This system really saves me time and energy when I'm planning.

Jill Potts, North Elementary
St. Peter, MN

Student Book Recommendations

Try this class library tip to help students select books to read. Glue a library card pocket to the inside back cover of each class library book. Then place an index card in each pocket. After a student has finished reading a book, he writes his comments about it on the card and places the card back in the pocket. Students will love sharing their opinions and reading those written by their classmates.

Susan Richardson, Snow Hill Elementary
Salisbury, MD

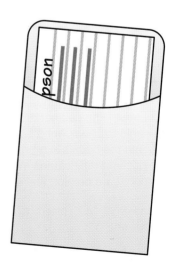

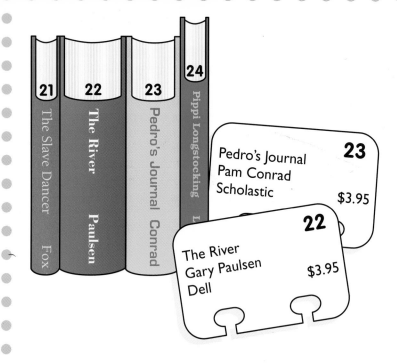

Classroom Library

Do you have trouble keeping track of the ever-growing number of books in your class library? Simplify your record keeping by assigning each book a number. Hold the book closed and write the number across the page edges at the top of the book. Arrange the books in numerical order. Record the title, author, publisher, cost, and assigned number for each book on individual Rolodex cards. Now the class librarian has only to scan the book tops to notice a missing book.

Virginia Hernandez-Gage
Kealing Junior High, Austin, TX

Keeping Up With Literature Books

It's quite a task for me to keep track of the many literature books that I use in my classroom. To organize them, I bought a Rolodex file in which to keep an inventory. On each separate Rolodex card, I list the title, author, reading level, number of copies, and location of a book. Instead of digging through my shelves to locate books, now I simply check my Rolodex. As another timesaver, I always stamp the inside cover of a new book when I add it to my Rolodex to indicate that the book is in my files. I also started filing my professional books, learning games, videos, and other learning materials on color-coded Rolodex cards. With my handy Rolodex, I can locate my teaching materials in a snap!

Kimberly VanHise—Grs. 4–6
Burns, OR

Check This Out!

Solve the mystery of managing your classroom library with this easy-to-use system. On each of several library-card pockets, write a range of alphabet letters, such as "A–F." Attach the pockets to the side of your filing cabinet or desk with magnetic tape. When a student wants to check out a book from your library, have him write his name and the book's title on an index card and then place the card in the pocket that includes the letter of his last name. The result is a classroom card catalog that's no mystery to manage!

Jill Lynn Perry—Gr. 5, Mason Corinth Elementary
Williamstown, KY

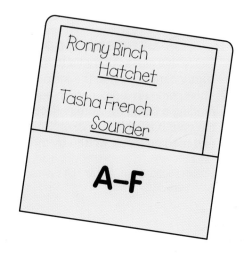

No Lockers? No Problem!

Without individual lockers or a coatroom, the storage area in our classroom (which included a shelved rack and a few coat hooks) always seemed to be littered with fallen backpacks, lunchboxes, and coats. To help organize our belongings, I brought coat hangers from home. Now students keep their coats on hangers hanging from the shelved rack. They put their backpacks on the coat hooks, and their hats, gloves, and lunches on the shelf. No more tripping over lunchboxes and backpacks!

Phyllis Ellett—Grs. 3–4 Multiage
Earl Hanson Elementary
Rock Island, IL

Desk Organizers

A student's desk can often be a disaster area. Books, notebooks, and pencil boxes take up a lot of space. Something as simple as Ziploc bags can help your students with organizational skills. They take up less space than pencil boxes, are inexpensive, and can be easily replaced. I keep a box of these bags on hand in my room. As the original boxes fall apart during the year, students can use the bags to separate and organize their markers, colored pencils, crayons, etc.

Lori Brandman—Gr. 5
Shallowford Falls Elementary, Marietta, GA

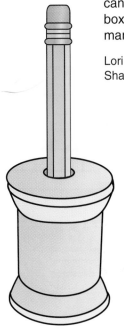

Anchor It With a Spool

Here's a crafty solution to the problem of misplaced pencils. Use Velcro to attach a wooden or Styrofoam thread spool to each student desk. These inexpensive spools are available at most craft and dime stores. Have pupils park their pencils in the spools when not in use.

Penny Parchem
Dallas, TX

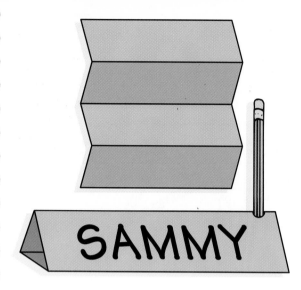

Double-Duty Nametags

These sturdy nametags also serve as handy pencil holders. For each nametag, fold a sheet of heavy paper twice to form four sections. Open the sheet; then overlap the two end sections and glue them together to make a base for the resulting triangular tube. Write the student's name on both sides of the nametag. Punch a hole for holding a pencil at the top of the nametag as shown. Helpful for substitutes too!

Cynthia E. Britton, Longley Way School
Arcadia, CA

Personalized Pencils

Even the most responsible student will sometimes ask to borrow a pencil. Instead of using valuable class time to give another lecture on being prepared, try this simple tip. At the beginning of the school year, order 100 inexpensive pencils printed with your name. Keep the pencils in a jar on your desk. Since the pencils are personalized with your name, students will be more likely to return them when they're done.

Judy O'Dell, Caddo Middle Magnet School
Shreveport, LA

Team Boxes

Save class time by simplifying the organization and distribution of materials during cooperative group activities. Provide each group with a shoebox or another lidded container. Stock each box with items such as scissors, pens, pencils, markers, colored pencils, tape, glue, rulers, and small notepads. Not only will precious time be saved when preparing for group activities, but team members will also learn to practice sharing and patience!

Deedra Bignar, Nebo Elementary
Jena, LA

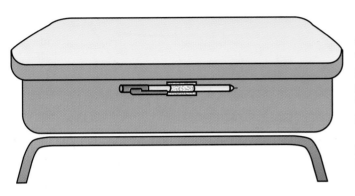

Handy Red Pens

What one tool has made more corrections than any other? The red pen, of course! Provide each student with his own pen for making corrections. Attach the rough side of sticky-back Velcro to the front of each student's desk; then attach the soft side to a red pen. When it's time to correct papers, students will always have marking pens right at their fingertips.

Lorri Burton—Gr. 5, Huddleston Elementary
Huddleston, VA

Lead Beds

Dull pencils don't slow my cooperative-learning groups down! Students begin each day with two sharp pencils. When a student's pencil point breaks or gets dull, he simply places his pencil in the "lead bed" located on his cooperative group's table. These "beds" are actually soup cans decorated with Con-Tact paper. A class helper sharpens the pencils at lunchtime and at the end of the day. Classwork stays neat and time is used effectively!

Shelly Zennon
Casa Grande, AZ

May I Borrow a Pencil?

If you often hear, "May I borrow a pencil?", here's an idea that will stop "lead lifters" in their tracks! Divide your class into teams; then select one person in each group to be the Supplies Steward. Put several pencils into a separate container for each team. (Try using empty coffee or frosting cans, baby wipes boxes, or large butter tubs.) Have each team decorate its container; then hold a contest to choose the winning design. Reward the winning team with a supply of seasonal pencils with which to stock its container. Hold each Supplies Steward accountable for his team's pencil supply. Rotate stewards weekly, and watch your students get the point about being responsible!

Pat Twohey—Gr. 4, Old County Road School
Smithfield, RI

Supplies for Team 6 Only

Classroom Materials

Emergency Packs

An emergency pack is just the thing for those students who run out of paper, pencils, or pens during a school day. Have each student bring in a Ziploc bag, five folded sheets of ruled paper, two sharpened new pencils, and a black pen. Place all of the items inside the bag. Affix a name label to the front of each student's bag. Add a note to the bag like the one shown. Keep the packs at your desk until a student needs an item. Then send the note inside the bag home as a reminder that the item needs to be replaced.

Michael Williquette—Grs. 5–6
Faith Baptist School
Beecher, WI

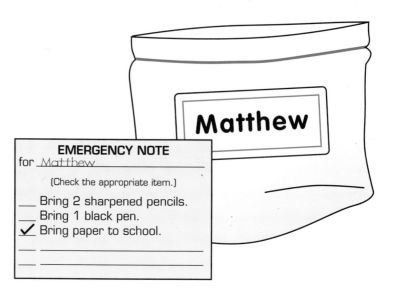

EMERGENCY NOTE
for _Matthew_
(Check the appropriate item.)
___ Bring 2 sharpened pencils.
___ Bring 1 black pen.
✓ Bring paper to school.
_____
_____

Borrowing Cards

Keep track of borrowed materials with this simple system. Have each child decorate a 5" x 7" index card with her name. Store each student's card in a clear plastic page protector that has been attached to the front of her desk. Whenever a student borrows a book or a supply item from another student or the teacher, she gives her borrowing card to the lender. The lender returns the card when the borrowed item is returned.

Shannon Renwick—Grs. 5–6, Peepeekisis Pesakastew School
Balcarres, Saskatchewan, Canada

Traveling Researchers

My students often go to the media center to research and compile reports. To avoid frequent trips back to the classroom for supplies, I purchased a three-tier basket cart on wheels. I filled the cart with scissors, crayons, a hole puncher, extra paper, and other necessary resources for the current project. Now this traveling resource center goes wherever my researchers go—saving us time and energy!

Marta Johnson—Gr. 4 , Haw Creek School
Asheville, NC

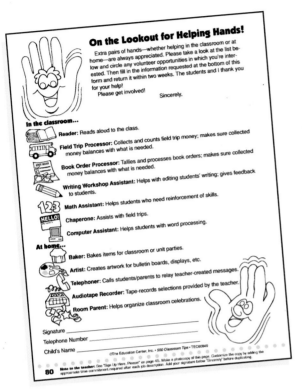

Sign Up Here, Please!

I like parent volunteers to help during the year. However, many parents are not sure what a job entails or the extent of involvement needed. In order to help parents decide what they can do to help, I developed a volunteer sign-up sheet (see page 80). It includes both classroom and at-home opportunities that are available, along with job descriptions. I distribute the sheets to students on the first day of school and ask that they be returned within two weeks. Parents like this informational sheet because it helps them know what they're getting into!

Maxine Pincott—Gr. 4, Oliver Ellsworth School
Windsor, CT

A Head Start on Next Year

Thanks to some advanced planning, I enjoyed a much smoother opening of school this year. At the end of last year, one of my parent volunteers duplicated supply lists, first-day fun sheets, get-acquainted activities, basic-facts homework sheets, and handouts for our first social studies unit. My students assembled and stapled packets for this year's students. Because of the head start I got in June, the beginning of this school year was a lot less hectic!

Linda Flagg—Gr. 4, Lithia, FL

Parent-Volunteer Notebook

I am always pleased to have parent volunteers help in the classroom. However, many times the helper comes while I am teaching a lesson, and I cannot stop to give her directions. I solved the problem by providing a special looseleaf notebook for my volunteers (see the sample notebook page). As soon as my helper enters the room, she goes to this notebook and signs her name next to a job. With my explanations always available in the book, the volunteer can get right to work without interrupting me while I'm teaching. Not all volunteers feel comfortable doing certain tasks. Offering them choices encourages these helpers to return to my classroom again.

Sandra P. Neuhauser—Gr. 4, Halethorpe Elementary
Randallstown, MD

Parent Volunteers

Parent Volunteers' Basket

When you find yourself spending too much time cutting out things, stapling packets, or publishing students' writings, just remember that parents love to help out! And having parents complete these tasks saves you valuable time. Just place the items that you need help with in a basket in your classroom, along with essentials such as scissors, markers, rulers, and a stapler. Everything will then be ready when a volunteer comes to your class. If you're in the middle of a lesson, you don't have to stop to explain what needs to be done. Parents will know to go to the basket and get started!

Debbie Schneck—Gr. 4, Fogelsville Elementary
Schnecksville, PA

"Working Parents" Club

To reduce my stress load, I delegate work to parents in my class. At the beginning of the school year, I send home a letter asking parents to join the Working Parents Club. The club is for parents who can't help in class during school hours. I send club members bulletin boards, learning centers, posters, games, and even book orders to work on at home. The parents return the items to school in about a week. This extra help gives me time to plan and evaluate student progress. Plus, working parents have the satisfaction of knowing they're making a contribution to their children's class. I even have time now to relax and look for new ideas in my latest issue of *The Mailbox* magazine!

Sara Partlow—Gr. 4, Virginia Run Elementary
Centreville, VA

Parents to the Rescue!

After trying to dig myself out of a continuous mountain of paperwork, it became obvious to me that the work was too much for one person. So I enlisted the help of parent volunteers. Before the start of each new month, I sent a Help Wanted note home with each child. From the responses, I created a volunteer schedule for that month, which I sent to those parents who had agreed to help. Some parents signed up for a regular spot at the beginning of the year and were "regulars." I trained these parents so that they were familiar with my filing system, computer programs, and other procedures. (Parent volunteers were not privy to confidential files, reports, or tests.) Many of my parents who worked outside the home even offered to do paperwork tasks for me in the evenings.

Stacy Barrett Stuttard—Gr. 4, Allegheny 1 School
Duncansville, PA

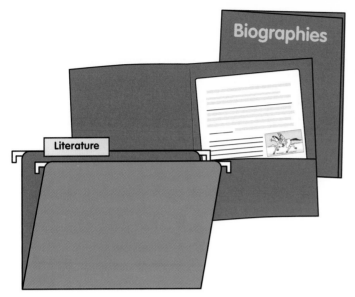

Color-Coded File Cabinet

Has your file cabinet become more of a dumping ground than a valuable organizational tool? If so, try this simple filing system. Purchase hanging file folders in different colors. Label each colored set with a subject such as Literature, Science, Seasonal Activities, and Administrative Information. Next, purchase pocket folders in the same colors as the hanging folders. Label the front of each folder with a specific topic such as Myths, Rocks and Minerals, and Valentine's Day. Use the right side of each folder to store information, reproducibles, forms, patterns, etc. As you use an item from the right pocket, transfer it to the left pocket. At a glance, you'll know what you've already used. And filing becomes a much easier, less bothersome task!

Lea Holton, Audubon Elementary
Louisville, KY

Double-Duty Plan Book

Say goodbye to your desk calendar with this "why-didn't-I-think-of-that?" timesaver! When you set up your lesson plan book, set aside the first and last columns. Label the first column "Calendar"; then use it to list parent conferences, school programs, standardized testing, and other special activities scheduled for each day. Title the last column "Reminders for Tomorrow." List in this column preparations for the next day, such as checking out video equipment, bringing doughnuts, or duplicating reproducibles. With this simple tip, you'll no longer need to keep a separate desk calendar.

Gratsiela Sabangan—Grs. 4–6
Three Angels School, Wichita, KS

Recycled File Folders

Recycle file folders with this clever money-saving idea. Gather a different-colored pad of self-sticking notes for each subject area, such as pink for reading, yellow for math, etc. Then place a brightly colored note on the tab of each folder. Write the label for that folder on the note as shown. When you no longer need a folder but want to reuse it, simply remove the note and add a new one.

Barbara Kenney—Gr. 4, Colo-NESCO Elementary
McCallsburg, IA

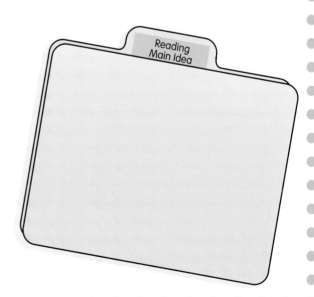

Planning and Filing

All in One Binder

Use a three-ring binder to keep your teacher essentials all in one place. Make a lesson plan template that includes your lunchtime, special times, and other weekly scheduled activities. Make several copies of the template; then place them in a three-ring binder with your grade book, stickers, grading scale, and other important information. Everything you need will be right at your fingertips!

Cathy Stemen, Cardington, OH

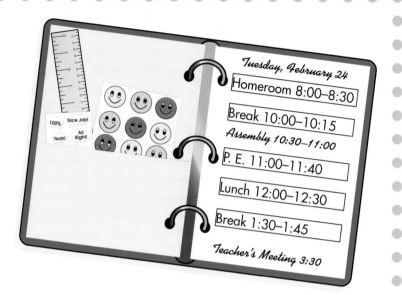

Glowing Originals

Giving out my original copies of materials to students was one of the mistakes I made during my first year of teaching. By the time I realized that a student had the original, it was too late. I solved this problem by using a yellow fluorescent highlighter to mark the bottom of each of my originals. The marking on the paper reminds me not to give out my copy. The marking is also invisible when duplicated, and my students know to return a sheet if it has a yellow block of color on it.

Kim C. Davis—Gr. 4, Fair Street Elementary
Gainesville, GA

Monthly Idea Binders

How can you organize the great teaching ideas you collect from various sources so they'll be easy to use? Put them in monthly binders! Purchase a three-ring binder for each school month. Add a tab to each binder for every subject taught: language arts, math, reading, social studies, science, writing, etc. Place calendars and holiday activities in the front of each binder. Then file all remaining ideas and activities by subject for quick reference. As each new month begins, just pull out that month's binder and you're ready to go!

Denise Menchaca—Grs. 3–5, Eastside Elementary
Brooksville, FL

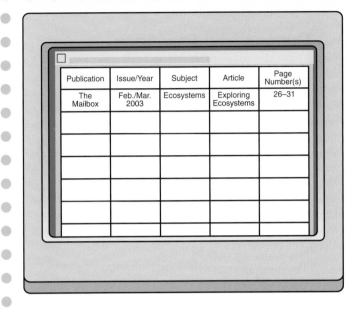

Publication	Issue/Year	Subject	Article	Page Number(s)
The Mailbox	Feb./Mar. 2003	Ecosystems	Exploring Ecosystems	26–31

Database Organizer

"Where did I see that neat activity?" If this sounds familiar, eliminate searching through magazines and books for lost ideas by creating your own computer database. Set up your database using fields titled "Publication," "Issue/Year," "Subject," "Article," and "Page Number(s)." As you look through a magazine or book, write the information needed on a sticky note attached to its front cover. Later, type the information from the note into the appropriate database fields. Whenever you need an idea on a specific topic, such as ecosystems, go to the Find command in the database and type ecosystems. The database will list the name of each idea you've entered, including the book/magazine featuring it and the page number on which it can be found. How simple, organized, and convenient!

Heather Dick, Woodsfield Elementary
Woodsfield, OH

Organized at Last!

Do you find it hard to keep up with your planbook and gradebook? I often find that I've grabbed the wrong one off my desk! To end this frustration, combine your gradebook and planbook into one notebook using a medium-size, three-ring binder. Carefully remove the pages from each book. Punch holes in the pages and insert them in the binder, using a divider to separate the two books. Adding a third section for staff-meeting agendas and other important notes is also helpful.

Erin Flint—Gr. 4
Cathedral of St. Peter School, Kansas City, KS

Filing by Colors

I put a large colored sticker on the front of each of my file cabinet drawers. I also put corresponding colored stickers on all of the alphabetized file folders that are stored in that drawer. My students are then able to help me refile any folders; at a glance, a student can tell in which drawer a file belongs. This not only provides me with valuable filing help, but the helpers also get alphabetizing practice!

Kathleen Jordan, Orange County Schools
Altamonte Springs, FL

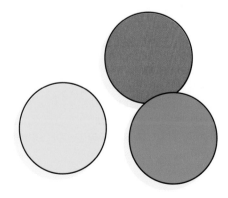

Customized Planbook

Creating your own personalized planbook is a snap! Begin by designing your own customized daily planbook page, filling in scheduled activities such as resource classes, lunchtime, bathroom breaks, and recess. Make enough copies of this sheet for a month. Then use a binding machine to attach decorative front and back covers to the sheets. You'll never have to worry about squeezing your lessons into a commercially made planbook again!

Diane R. Highlander—Gr. 4, Columbus Elementary
Edwardsville, IL

Year-Round Self-Evaluation

As I complete lessons or units of study throughout the year, I find myself wanting to add to, delete from, or change my teaching methods. To make sure that I will remember my ideas when the next year rolls around, I take a moment to jot them down on the blank pages at the front of my plan book. Come September, I review my list of ideas and get ready to implement them. It's an easy, painless way to evaluate and improve my teaching methods from year to year.

Kate Luchtel—Tutor K–8, Gardena Valley Christian School
Gardena, CA

Quick Plans

Want to make writing lesson plans practically painless? I purchase a three-ring binder, a supply of photo album filler pages (each of which holds six 3" x 5" photographs), and six different-colored packs of 3" x 5" index cards. Next, I assign each subject area a different color. On the front of each card, I write a lesson's objective and assignment. On the back, I list the materials and directions. Then I slide the six cards into the slots of one album page. If I get behind in a lesson, I just pull out that card and move it to another day's page. No more erasing, whiting out, or crossing out big blocks in my planbook. At the end of the month, I pull out the cards and store them in a file box for next year.

Kim Brown—Gr. 4
Bixby, OK

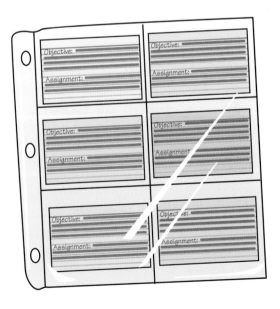

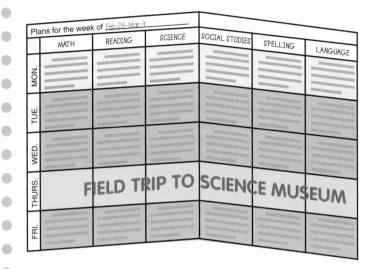

	MATH	READING	SCIENCE	SOCIAL STUDIES	SPELLING	LANGUAGE
MON.						
TUE.						
WED.						
THURS.	FIELD TRIP TO SCIENCE MUSEUM					
FRI.						

Plans for the week of Feb. 28–Mar. 4

Color-Coded Planbook

Color-coding my planbook keeps me aware of special holidays and changes in the calendar months. I highlight each new month in a different color (September in red, October in orange, etc.). Special school event days get their own hues. These different colors alert me to calendar changes that occur in the middle of the week so that I can put up new bulletin boards and seasonal decorations.

Denell Hilgendorf—Grs. 1–6, Osaka International School
Osaka, Japan

Lesson-Plan Highlights

Help prepare for the day's lessons with this bright idea! Use a highlighter marker to highlight the items in your planbook that need to be duplicated, prepared in advance, or purchased. You'll know at a glance what needs to be done for each day's lessons.

Patty J. Vermeer—Gr. 4, Galva-Holstein Elementary
Holstein, IA

Grade-Recording Hint

I've developed a color-code system for my gradebook to help me keep track of students' work. I draw a black box around a late assignment, a red box around a late assignment due to an absence, and a green box around a "do-over" assignment. At a glance, I know which students have late assignments and those who need to redo an assignment in order to receive a passing grade.

Vicki Steh—Gr. 4, Stettin Elementary School
Wausau, WI

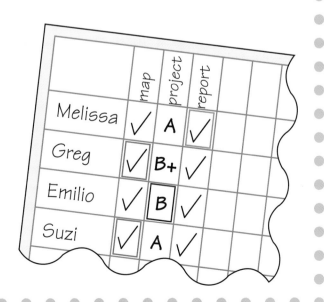

	map	project	report
Melissa	✓	A	✓
Greg	✓	B+	✓
Emilio	✓	B	✓
Suzi	✓	A	✓

Planning and Filing

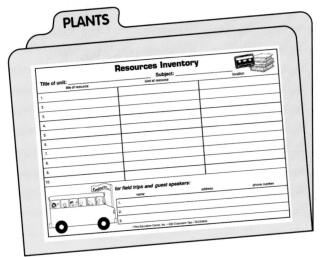

Unit Resources at Your Fingertips

Whenever you begin teaching a new unit, do you forget where you stored a favorite poster or video? Or you remember that your students did a fun project, but you can't recall what it was? You probably already have a file folder with materials for each unit that you teach. To help you keep track of items that won't fit in a folder, make a copy of the reproducible on page 81 and paste it to the front of your unit folder. Use this form to list favorite items to include with the unit and—most importantly—where they can be located. Also list contact information for guest speakers and field trips, including their names, addresses, and phone numbers. Laminate the folder for durability. When you want to add new items to the list, just use an extra-fine permanent marker.

Dawn Helton, Evadale Elementary
Evadale, TX

Missing-Assignments Notebook

Tracking missed assignments is hassle-free with this management technique. Write "Missing Assignments" on the cover of a spiral notebook. In alphabetical order, write the name of a different student at the top of each notebook page. Keep the notebook at your desk. Whenever a student fails to turn in an assignment, list it on his page. When the assignment is turned in, cross it out.

Doreen Placko—Gr. 5, St. Patrick School, Wadsworth, IL

Wading Through Paperwork

Are you overwhelmed by the assortment of paper that piles up on your desk each week? I have discovered an easy way to get organized. I purchased a wire hanging file to place on my desk. I then labeled eight hanging folders with the days of the week, "Book Orders," "To Copy," and "Monthly Activities and Clip Art." In the hanging folder for each day of the week, I have a manila file folder for each subject—Spelling, Math, Social Studies, Reading, etc. When I plan my lessons, I pull the activities that I will need and place them in the folder for the day they will be used. I then know what copies I need to make on Friday to prepare for the upcoming week. I love coming to school on Monday morning knowing that I'm organized and have everything ready to go!

Sheila K. Bowman—Gr. 4, Victory Christian School
Albuquerque, NM

Ideas in a Flash

Have you ever run across a great idea in a magazine and then later gone back and been unable to find it when you needed it most? If so, you'll want to try this handy tip for organizing your favorite ideas. Cut out interesting ideas as you read through your favorite magazines. Label different sections of a magnetic photo album with headings such as arts and crafts, behavior management, math, reading, organizational tips, etc. Place each idea in the photo album under the plastic page covering—there's no need to paste. Then, when you need an idea, all you have to do is flip to the appropriate section in the album. No more looking around in vain for those misplaced ideas!

Sharon Zacharda—Gr. 4, West View Elementary
Pittsburgh, PA

Monthly Book Tip

Never miss out on another great monthly idea again with this simple tip! Duplicate the table of contents from each of your monthly idea books; then attach it to the planbook page for a week or more before the new month begins. The copy will remind you to pull your book to find ideas for the upcoming month. You'll have plenty of time to copy worksheets, gather supplies, and make new bulletin boards. Plus, by the end of the month, you'll have a ready-made monthly unit for next year!

Sharon Abell
Winston-Salem, NC

Monthly Folders

Organize your seasonal and monthly activities with this simple tip. Purchase 12 brightly colored two-pocket folders. Create a computer-generated cover for each month as shown. Glue it to the front of a folder. Then laminate the folder. Store teacher ideas and materials for that month in the left-hand pocket. In the right-hand pocket, place student reproducibles and activities. With the folder for the month in hand, your ideas are ready to use!

Kelly Fornauf—Gr. 5, Northwestern Lehigh Middle School
New Tripoli, PA

Lesson-Planning Timesaver

Save tons of time when writing weekly plans with this timesaving tip. Hole-punch a sheet of acetate and place it in your planning binder. Copy the classes, events, or specials that occur at scheduled times each week onto the acetate. Cut windows in the acetate where you need to write plans that change daily or weekly. When the week ends, just take the acetate from the binder and move it to the next week's planning page. Then all you have to do is fill in the windows with your plans.

Laurie Kowalke, Fairfield Center School
Baraboo, WI

Subject: Time:	Reading 8:00–9:00	Language Arts 9:00–10:00	Math 10:00–11:00	Lunch 11:00–11:30
MONDAY				
TUESDAY	Bus Duty	Music		
WEDNESDAY	P. E.			

Planning as You Go

Take a little time now to save lots of planning time later. Staple copies of the reproducibles used each day directly to that dated page in your planbook. Also jot down notes about any changes you'd like to make in the lessons. When making next year's plans, you can look back at the reproducibles, read your notes, and prepare your lessons in a snap!

Sharon Abell
Winston-Salem, NC

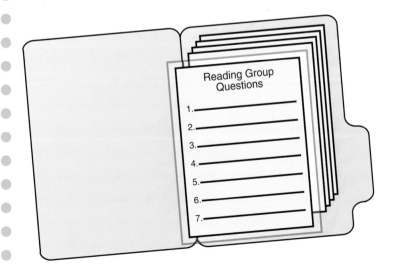

Reading Group
Questions
1.
2.
3.
4.
5.
6.
7.

Five In From the End

Eliminate the problem of running out of classroom forms and worksheets with this easy idea. Laminate one copy of each reproducible you use for games, reading, group work, etc.; then place it in the proper file folder five in from the end. When a student goes to get a reproducible from a folder and sees that the next one is the laminated sheet, instruct him to place it on your desk. Not only will the laminated sheet signal you to run off more copies, but there will also still be some reproducibles left in the folder for other students to grab that day.

Barbara Wilkes Delnero—Gr. 4
Tuckerton Elementary, Tuckerton, NJ

					TEST
Jon	89		79		100
Sue	72		85		90
Kisha	91		95		100
Ricky	100		90		80
Alan	84		92		100
Kim	90		100		90

Gradebook Gimmicks

Eliminate the problem of eyestrain from trying to read small gradebook boxes with these "A+" ideas! To create extra space, skip a line after every three or four names in your gradebook. Avoid confusing student scores by skipping every other line when entering grades. Make averaging scores easier by highlighting grades for tests/reports and semester averages in different colors. Soon sore eyes will become a thing of the past!

Sharon Zacharda—Gr. 4, West View Elementary
Pittsburgh, PA

File-Box Plans

Whenever my school system adopts a new textbook, I label a small index card with each chapter title. On each chapter card, I list the topics and page numbers that I plan to use. I also list workbook pages and other projects that I like to include in my units. On the back of the card, I add audiovisual materials and library books that I need for that chapter. I keep these cards filed in a small box on my desk. Each week when it's time to write lesson plans, I turn to my card file instead of dragging out those huge teacher manuals. Now I rarely forget projects, filmstrips, or books that I enjoy using!

Holly Bates—Gr. 4, Arlington Elementary
Anson, ME

Ready-to-Go Planbook

Setting up your planbook can be very time consuming. To save time, make a couple of computer-generated sheets of labels for each subject area—plus lunch, recess, art, gym, music, and other activities. Also include the time for each item on its label, as well as a small, colorful picture to make the label more noticeable. Attach these labels in the appropriate boxes for each week's lesson plans. Then, when you get ready to complete your lesson plans, you won't have to recopy all of the subjects and their time periods.

Kathleen Lynch—Gr. 4, St. Aloysius School
Jackson, NJ

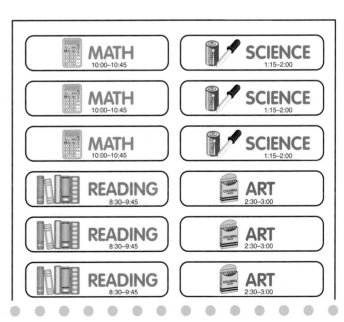

MATH 10:00–10:45	SCIENCE 1:15–2:00
MATH 10:00–10:45	SCIENCE 1:15–2:00
MATH 10:00–10:45	SCIENCE 1:15–2:00
READING 8:30–9:45	ART 2:30–3:00
READING 8:30–9:45	ART 2:30–3:00
READING 8:30–9:45	ART 2:30–3:00

Reproducibles at My Fingertips

To help me keep up with my favorite reproducibles, I store them in three-ring binders. Each subject-area binder has dividers labeled with skills, such as "Context Clues," "Synonyms," "Homonyms," "Creative Writing," etc. When a student needs extra practice with a particular skill, I simply flip to an appropriate reproducible and copy it for her immediate use.

Cynthia T. Reeves—Gr. 4, Albert Harris Elementary
Martinsville, VA

Daily Work Folders

Here's a colorful way to arrange your daily materials. Label each of five different-colored folders with a day of the week. Inside each folder place worksheets, ideas, or activities planned for that day. Store the folders where they can be easily reached. On the specified day, use the materials inside each folder. To plan ahead, make folders for a two-week period.

Betty Adams—Gr. 5, Staunton Elementary
Staunton, IN

Planbook Organization

Are you tired of rewriting time schedules and repetitive information each week in your planbook? If so, buy a package of mailing address labels from an office supply store. Be sure to purchase labels that can be run through a copying machine. Type your schedules and other information that is the same each week onto a master sheet. Then copy the sheet onto the labels. Cut to fit into your planbook. Peel the labels and attach to your planbook pages. No more copying the same info week after week!

Sheryl Phelps, Image Elementary
Vancouver, WA

MONDAY	TUESDAY	WEDNESDAY	THURSD
Music 8:00–8:30			
	Library 9:00–9:30		

Apple Organizer

Searching for a way to get some paper off your desk? I use a hot-glue gun to attach several clothespins to a red poster board apple. I then hang the apple on a classroom wall within reach of my students. Each clothespin holds items that students frequently need: attendance forms, library passes, lunch forms, announcements, etc. My apple organizer frees up space on my desk and saves students time when they need these items.

Brenda Ramsey, Foley Middle School, Berea, KY

Bind It!

Does keeping up with your monthly materials have you in a bind? Purchase and label one binder for each month of the school year. Place all your ideas, reproducibles, and bulletin board materials (placed inside hole-punched Ziploc bags) for each month in one of the binders. Use dividers to separate the materials inside each binder. Now your materials will be easily accessible and organized!

Tanya Glaser—Grs. 5–6 Special Education
Millard Fillmore Elementary
Moravia, NY

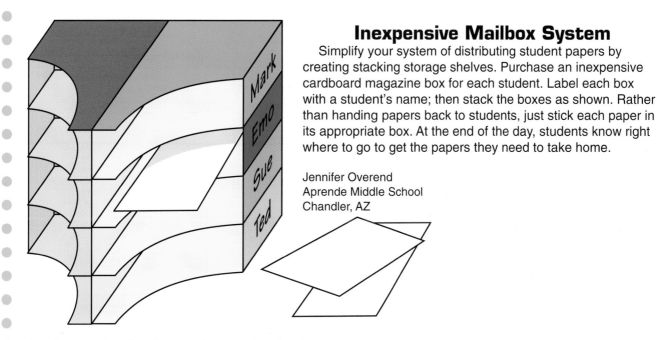

Inexpensive Mailbox System

Simplify your system of distributing student papers by creating stacking storage shelves. Purchase an inexpensive cardboard magazine box for each student. Label each box with a student's name; then stack the boxes as shown. Rather than handing papers back to students, just stick each paper in its appropriate box. At the end of the day, students know right where to go to get the papers they need to take home.

Jennifer Overend
Aprende Middle School
Chandler, AZ

Planning and Filing

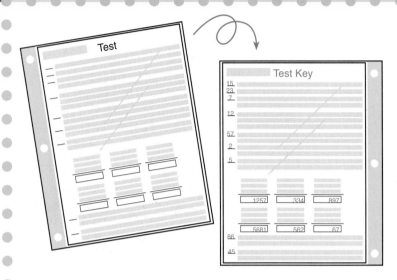

Test Key Notebooks

If you have trouble keeping test keys at your fingertips, try this. Purchase a three-ring notebook for each subject. Use clear plastic page protectors to fill each binder. Then place all original tests and their keys inside the page protectors. Problem solved!

Beverly Langland—Gr. 5
Trinity Christian Academy
Jacksonville, FL

Pile Stoppers

To keep the stress down, I have to keep the mess down! It's easy to let the countless memos, sticky notes, parent letters, and catalogs pile up on my desk, tables, or counters. To free myself from this paper burden, I immediately throw out anything I know I'll never *really* read. After reading the "must-read" items, I make a note on my calendar of anything I need to remember from the item read; then I toss it into the trash can too.

Another trick I've learned is to file instead of pile! I keep a stack of manila folders handy on my desk. Each time I receive a piece of paper that I want to keep, I quickly make a new file or drop the item into an existing file. These "pile stoppers" help keep things off my desk *and* my mind!

Kate Newton-Redwood, Grants-Pass, OR

Answer Key Tip

Whenever I duplicate a worksheet, I always make two extra copies for my files. One copy becomes my duplicating master. After making an answer key on the second copy, I staple it to the back of the master. I never have to search for answer keys or books that have the answers I need.

Jane O. Shapiro
Charlotte A. Dunning School
Framingham, MA

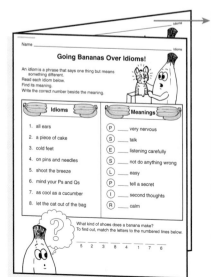

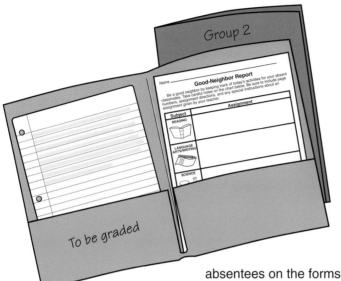

Group Folders

To help handle the daily paperwork involved in teaching, I use colorful pocket folders. Each group in my class is assigned a specific colored folder. The left pocket of each group's folder holds work that students turn in to be graded. At the end of the day, I check the folders for these assignments. The right pocket is for graded work that I return to students. It also contains forms on which the group's leader writes absentees' assignments.

Before class, I place each group folder on a group member's desk. This student is responsible for the folder during class. The folder contains reproducibles or other materials for the class. The student in charge distributes materials, writes absentees' names on their reproducibles, and writes assignments for any absentees on the forms provided. This relieves me of having to save reproducibles and copy assignments for absentees. Students remove graded papers or absentee assignments daily so they don't accumulate in the folder. This simple system saves me tons of time and easily keeps the mountain of paperwork organized.

Cyndee Knock—Gr. 5, Windermere Elementary, Austin, TX

Supplementary Filmstrips

My school library recently received an assortment of filmstrips that correlate with our new social studies book. Rather than simply file the list of these filmstrips, I made a copy and cut apart the individual filmstrip names and descriptions. I then went through the social studies teacher's text and taped each filmstrip information strip to the appropriate unit page. Now when I prepare to teach that particular unit, I'll know that a supplemental filmstrip is available.

Mary Dinneen, Mountain View School, Bristol, CT

Snappy Seasonal Sayings

Each time I comb through a teacher's magazine and note a catchy saying, I jot it down on a notecard labeled with a month, season, or subject; then I place the card in a special file. Later, when I need a creative title for an activity or bulletin board, I pull one from the file. No longer do I have to rack my brain for that snappy saying to liven up my classroom!

Othelia Miller—Chapter I Migrant
Brewster USD 314
Brewster, KS

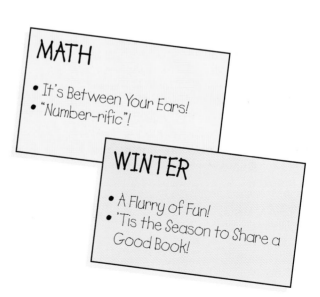

Planning and Filing

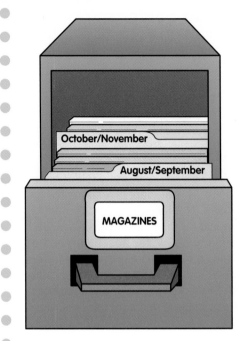

Magazine Storage

All of my teacher magazines were once stored in a drawer in random order. Every time I needed a certain unit or idea, I'd have to dig through all of the magazines to find what I needed. Since this was such a waste of time, I decided to organize the magazines into bimonthly categories. I made dividers out of heavy cardboard, labeling them "August/ September," "October/November," etc. Now it's so much easier to locate what I'm looking for!

Mary Dinneen
Mountain View School
Bristol, CT

Oldies but Goodies

At the end of the school year, I like to organize all of the wonderful ideas I have received from magazines such as *The Mailbox*® all year long. From each issue, I compile all of the teaching tips, units, and activities that I have found useful, and I make one photocopy of each needed reproducible. Next, I organize the material and reproducibles into hanging file folders that are labeled according to seasons, holidays, subject matter, etc. I like to hang my files in a plastic crate that is inexpensive and easy to transport.

Lisa Chotto—Grs. 4–8
Elmwood Academy
Terrytown, LA

Clearly Organized

See your way through to better organization with the following idea. Sort your overhead transparencies by subject or topic; then punch three holes in each. Place the transparencies in a three-ring binder behind subject dividers. From now on, finding the right transparency for the job will be a breeze.

Andrea A. Murray
Munford Middle School
Munford, TN

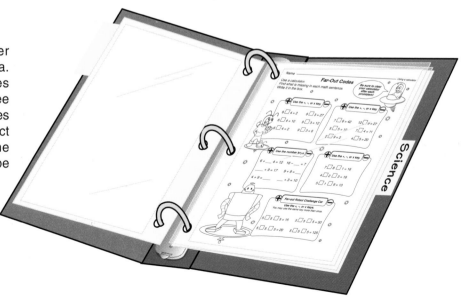

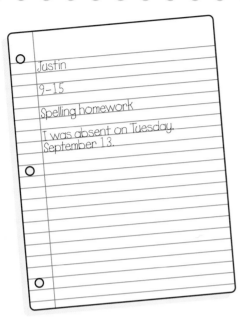

Justin

9-15

Spelling homework

I was absent on Tuesday, September 13.

"Gimme" One of Three, Please!

If you've got lots of kids and lots of papers to grade, it's often easy to be in the dark about whether a student was absent or just didn't do an assignment. Solve this challenge by asking each student to hand in one of the following each time you collect a homework assignment:

- the homework assignment
- a sheet of paper labeled with the student's name, the date, the assignment name, and the phrase "I was absent on [the date the student missed school]."
- a sheet of paper labeled with the student's name, the date, the assignment name, and the phrase "I did not complete [name of assignment]."

File any "I did not complete…" papers to use during student and parent conferences.

Patricia E. Dancho, Apollo-Ridge Middle School
Spring Church, PA

Catalog Orders...Ready to Mail

Do you spend hours each spring poring over catalogs looking for things you want to order for the following school year? Whenever you see something you want, go ahead and write up a purchase order and save it in a file. Near the end of the year when your principal asks for requests, just open up the file and look over your purchase orders. Check to be sure you're within budget; then submit the orders. You'll save a lot of time formerly spent looking for (and trying to remember!) things you saw throughout the year and wanted to order.

Jane O. Shapiro
Charlotte A. Dunning School
Framingham, MA

Late Assignment Solution

It's probably happened to you before: A student turns work in late only to claim later that it was submitted on time. Eliminate this problem with the help of a dated rubber stamp (like those used in most libraries). Simply stamp the date on all assignments as soon as they're turned in. Problem solved!

Judy O'Dell
Caddo Middle Magnet School
Shreveport, LA

Finished? Check It Off!

Use this handy tip and with one glance you'll identify which students have turned in an assignment. Make a supply of assignment forms similar to the one shown. Store the forms and a few two-pocket folders where students typically turn in their work. The first student to turn in a specific assignment fills out the top portion of a form and clips it to the front of a folder. As each student turns in her assignment, she places her work inside the folder and initials next to her name. Simple!

Lynsia Sprouse—Gr. 5
Booker Independent School District
Booker, TX

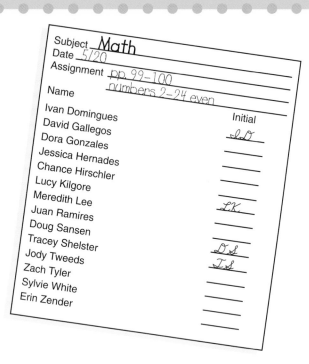

Subject **Math**
Date 5/20
Assignment pp. 99–100
numbers 2–24 even

Name   Initial

Ivan Domingues
David Gallegos
Dora Gonzales   I.D
Jessica Hernades
Chance Hirschler
Lucy Kilgore
Meredith Lee   LK
Juan Ramires
Doug Sansen
Tracey Shelster   D.S
Jody Tweeds   I.S
Zach Tyler
Sylvie White
Erin Zender

Timesaving Folder System

Student papers used to litter my desk. Some needed grading; some needed corrections; others had to be filed. To spread the workload around, I placed a folder for each student in a plastic tub. In the morning each child removed his folder from the tub. During the day, the student placed any "work in progress" or papers needing corrections inside his folder. When time permitted, he worked to complete any items in his folder. At the end of the day, my students and I prioritized their work for the next day; those papers needing attention first were placed at the front of each child's folder. As students left, they placed their folders alphabetically in the tub. With just a quick flip through the tub, I could check my students' progress, insert extra practice activities in needed folders, or surprise students with a fun reproducible for the next day.

Nancy Niemants, Franklin School, Boone, IA

Sally
Theo
Jill
Ned
Alison
Bethany
Zach

Homework Organizer

Avoid the paper chase that homework can sometimes create with this tip. Type a class list and make copies. Each time you collect homework, place a copy of the list atop the papers. Then follow these steps:

1. Cross out the names of students who turned in the assignment.
2. Highlight the names of students who didn't turn in the assignment.
3. Paper-clip the list to the top of the papers.
4. Label the list with grades as you assess the work.
5. Transfer the grades to your gradebook.

Keep the list until Friday so you can refer to it when informing students about who owes work for the week.

Jennifer Peterman, Eli Whitney Elementary, Stratford, CT

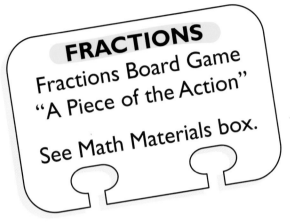

FRACTIONS

Fractions Board Game
"A Piece of the Action"

See Math Materials box.

Rolodex Organizer

Keeping track of all of your teaching materials can be a snap when you use a Rolodex flip file. List your materials on the Rolodex cards; then use highlighter pens to color-code the cards according to subject. Arrange the cards alphabetically by subject. When you're looking for that terrific poster on wetlands or the board game on fractions, the answer to "Where is it?" will be right at your fingertips!

Cathy Ogg—Gr. 4
Happy Valley Elementary
Johnson City, TN

Lesson Plan Timesaver

Sometimes the smallest tip can save a mountain of time! As I write my future lesson plans, I highlight all materials that will be used, such as handouts, art supplies, videos, etc. Then, as I look over the plans for the next day, I can see at a glance what materials I need to have ready. This simple idea also helps me to organize much more quickly when I have an unexpected need for a substitute teacher.

Nancy Niemants, Franklin Elementary, Boone, IA

Helpful Homework Tracking System

Tired of trying to keep track of students' missing homework? I created this easy system to make record keeping simpler. I fill a three-ring binder with a separate page for each student. If a student does not have a homework assignment when we begin checking the work, he finds his page in the binder and records the missing assignment along with the date and his signature. This binder allows me to check student progress at a glance and serves as a great resource during parent conferences. It has also helped me keep on top of things and reinforces the importance of completing homework to my students.

Joey

Math p. 12 10–20 Joey

Charlotte A. Lashley-Soto—Gr. 5
Jennie Reid Elementary, La Porte, TX

Seating Arrangements

Creative Desk Arrangement

Using clustering, I've arranged my students' desks in an interesting and efficient manner. Each cluster consists of six desks arranged around a central supply desk (see the illustration). The supply desk—which holds dictionaries, pencils, paper, and other materials—is adjusted two to five inches lower than the others. This classroom arrangement has several advantages:

- Students' personal comfort zones are staggered, yet cooperative learning is manageable.
- Often-used materials are easily accessible.
- Less space is used than in conventional arrangements.
- Students' elbows don't bump into each other!

Jeff Renfrow—Gr. 4
Entz Elementary
Mesa, AZ

Desk Clusters

Turn your students' desks into a handy teaching tool! Cluster most of your desks in groups of two, three, or four. Assign students to clusters with others who are working on similar material. Keep a couple of single desks for students who need time to work alone. During certain periods of the day, allow students to move to different desk clusters to get help from classmates while you teach small groups. With this plan, students have easy access to their peers without interrupting your instructional sessions.

Phyllis Ellett—Grs. 3–4 Multiage, Earl Hanson Elementary, Rock Island, IL

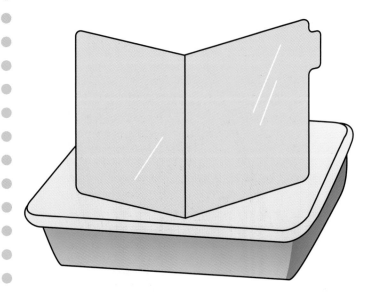

Cooperative-Group Test Taking

If your students' desks are arranged in cooperative groups, there's no need to move them into rows on test days. Instead, provide each student with a colorful laminated file folder (a different color for each group) to stand on her desktop for privacy. After a student finishes a test and turns it facedown on her desk, have her close the folder and put it in her desk. Not only does this method give students the privacy they need while taking a test, but it also lets you know at a glance when everyone is finished.

Penny Morrison
DAR Middle School
Grant, AL

A Desktag for Four

I teach four different groups of children each day. To keep track of seating, I made unique desktags. First, I laminated four different colors of construction paper. I then cut a class set of strips from each color of paper. The sets were of four different lengths: four inches, 4½ inches, five inches, and 5½ inches. I wrote my first group's names on the four-inch strips, my second group's names on the 4½-inch strips, etc. A set of four different-colored strips was then placed in a library card pocket (see illustration). Pockets were attached to desks with packaging tape.

When a student finds something left in a desk, he can look at the names to see who sat there before him and return the item to its owner. If a desk is messy after a class, I always know who is responsible. And if someone becomes too chatty in class, that person and his name strip are easily moved!

Louann Campbell—Gr. 5
Jane Robin Ellis Elementary
Arlington, TX

Seat Shuffle

Give students the chance to work with a variety of classmates using this simple seat shuffle. Number each group of desks in your room; then place a different-colored sticky dot on each desk in a group. From construction paper, cut sets of squares that match the colors on each group's desks. Write one table number per square until every desk in each group is represented. On Friday have students draw their seating assignments for the next week. With this quick shuffle, you can say goodbye to the negative behavior that often results from sitting with the same classmates week after week!

Christina Jepson—Gr. 5
Gateway Elementary
Travelers Rest, SC

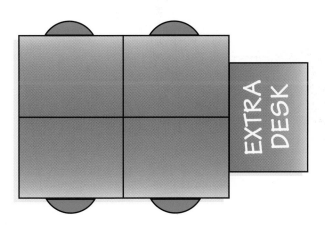

The Storage Desk

One obstacle to organization is a cluttered desk. But what does a student do when he has more supplies than storage space? Solve this problem by arranging student desks in groups of four. Place an extra empty desk at the end of each arrangement as shown. Encourage students to use this desk as an overflow area for supplies that don't fit in their own desks. Bye-bye, clutter!

Phyllis Ellett—Grs. 3–4 Multiage, Earl Hanson Elementary
Rock Island, IL

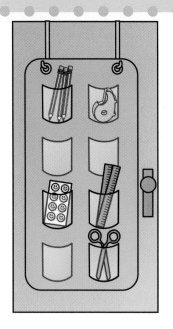

Shoe Bag Space Saver

If you are short on time and space in your classroom, try this. Purchase a shoe bag with clear plastic pockets. Hang it over a closet door in the classroom. Stickers, tape, staples, extra pencils, rulers, and other supplies can be stored in the pockets. The clear pockets make it easy to see what's stored inside.

Amy Beth O'Brien—Substitute
Truman Elementary
Lafayette, LA

Storing Portfolios

As any teacher who uses portfolios will agree, making them easily accessible to teachers, students, and parents is critical. One way that I've accomplished this is to divide my class into four groups. Each group is assigned a color. A colored box for each group is placed in each corner of the room. Portfolios are stored in colored file folders in the boxes. With this color-coded system, our portfolios are always easy to locate and grab at a moment's notice.

Pam Wardle—Gr. 5, Seattle Hill Elementary, Snohomish, WA

Chart and Poster Notebook

Organize your charts and posters in a snap! Begin by sorting charts and posters by subject. Take a picture of each; then mount the photos in a notebook, divided and labeled by subject. Store the charts and posters in a large flat box, one for each subject area. When it's time to teach a new lesson, you'll have a quick reference of the materials you have on hand.

Sherri Roberts—Gr. 4
Roosevelt Traditional School
Hutchinson, KS

Fast-Food Calculator Caddies

If you love french fries, you'll love gathering materials for this calculator storage idea! Collect a fast-food french fry container for each calculator. Cover each container's logo with a hamburger cutout. Write a student name or number on each cutout. Arrange the calculator caddies on a bulletin board using thumbtacks.

Melissa Kienzl
Eldred Elementary
Kunkletown, PA

Share Cart

To help organize my supplies, I've purchased a plastic storage cart on wheels. The upper part of the cart—intended for hanging file folders—makes a wonderful storage area for scissors, glue, staplers, crayons, and other classroom supplies. The lid on the cart helps keep the materials intact and in good condition. There are two sliding plastic trays at the bottom of the cart, perfect for keeping art and construction paper. My students love the fact that the cart can be moved around the room, making materials more accessible. Now I don't have to run back and forth to my desk to get supplies when I need them!

Angela Curry
Emory H. Markle Intermediate School
Hanover, PA

Storage Idea

To reduce the clutter of bulletin board letters in my closet, I put each set of letters in a Ziploc bag. I then punched a small hole in the side of each bag and hung it on a hook in my closet. Now I can easily find the letters I need.

Cathy Ogg—Gr. 4, Happy Valley Elementary
Johnson City, TN

Bulletin Board Letters File

Organize your bulletin-board letters with this easy idea. Obtain a file or large recipe box with alphabetical dividers. Put all the *A*s behind the *A* divider, the *B*s behind the *B* divider, and so on. Your letters will be right at your fingertips and easy to find when you need them!

Patty J. Vermeer—Gr. 4
Galva-Holstein Elementary
Holstein, IA

On the Ball With Organization

Want to be on the ball when it comes to organizing your supplies? Ask students to save the clear plastic containers in which tennis balls are packaged. Use the containers to organize your desk items and art supplies—rubber bands, tacks, paper clips, beads, buttons, etc. Since the containers are clear, you'll be able to find exactly what you need in a flash. What a simple way to guarantee you'll be an ace at organization!

Cynthia F. Acierto
Kalihi-Kai Elementary
Honolulu, HI

Simple Storage for Seasonal Essentials

Organize those monthly and seasonal bulletin boards and activities with these sturdy pockets. Use either extra large bulletin board oaktag folded in half, or two sheets of poster board. Staple together all but the top sides to create a large pocket. Label the contents on the outside of the pocket. For smaller items and monthly masters/handouts, staple the sides of a legal-size manila folder, leaving the top open. Store the smaller folders in the larger monthly pockets. Place all items together in a sturdy box that's been decorated by your students.

Theresa Azzolino
Washington School
Lodi, NJ

Simple Sticker Storage

Solve the sticky problem of sticker storage with this organizational tip! Take advantage of your summer months to transform a greeting card organizer into a handy tool for sorting and storing stickers. Use each month's individual pocket to store stickers for that month or season. Relabel the summer months' pockets for specific themes or curriculum areas, such as "Oceans" or "Math." Place grading or reward stickers in any unlabeled pockets. By getting organized over the summer, your stickers will be ready to use throughout the coming school year.

Patricia A. Faria
St. Angela School
Mattapan, MA

Two Scoops of Organization

Searching for an easy, inexpensive way to keep a unit organized? Cut off one side panel from a large cereal box. Then tape the box ends closed. Your unit will fit nicely into the box, which can be easily stored inside a filing cabinet drawer or on a shelf until you need it.

Sharon Zacharda—Gr. 4
West View Elementary
Pittsburgh, PA

Cardboard Paper Dividers

Here's a real timesaver for storing colored 12" x 18" construction paper. Instead of stacking one color on top of the other, stand the sheets on their sides. Organize the paper by color, separating each hue with heavy cardboard that has been cut into 12" x 18" sheets. Individual sheets will be easy to spot, and papers will slide out easily.

Mary Dinneen
Mountain View School, Bristol, CT

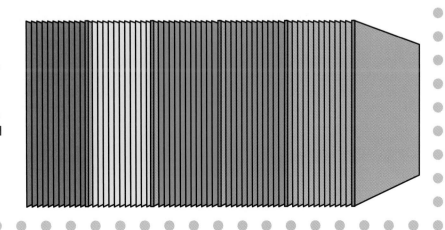

Great Greetings!

Ease your student teacher's first-day jitters by welcoming her with a student-made banner. A few days before the student teacher arrives, use a desktop publishing program to make a banner, or have students design their own special banner welcoming her. Have each student sign the banner; then hang it in the front of your classroom.

Kelly A. Wong, Berlyn School
Ontario, CA

Introductory Bulletin Board

Looking for a unique way to introduce your student teacher to your class? Have him create an autobiographical bulletin board to share with your students. Encourage the student teacher to use the bulletin board space to create a personal collage featuring pictures, mementos, and important information about his life. Provide time for the student teacher to discuss the bulletin board with students and answer questions.

Deborah Abrams Burroughs—Gr. 5, Laguna Elementary, Laguna, NM

Student Teacher Survival Kit

This easy-to-make kit is sure to get your student teacher off to a great start! Cover a shoebox with brightly colored Con-Tact paper; then apply apple or other school-related stickers. Next, write "Student Teacher Survival Kit" on the box lid. Place an assortment of handy items inside the box, such as a grader, red pens, incentive stickers, Band-Aid bandages, pencils, Life Savers candies, safety pins, a sewing kit, and a packet of aspirin. Give the box to your student teacher at your first meeting to start the experience off on a positive note!

Sandra Wilkin—Gr. 4
Parkview Elementary, Jackson, OH

A Warm and Fuzzy Welcome

Roll out the welcome mat for your student teacher with these easy ideas. Assign several students to set up a desk or working area for your student teacher. Have the students design a nametag for the student teacher and attach it to the desk. Then have them stock the desk with supplies, such as pencils and pens, paper, a planbook, and a class list and seating chart. Add additional comforts, such as a coffee mug filled with mints or a small floral arrangement. Once the student teacher arrives, assign several students to give her a guided tour of your school. These simple gestures are sure to leave your student teacher feeling more than welcome in her new surroundings!

Kimberly A. McCormick
Wilmington Area Middle School
New Castle, PA

The Perfect Pick-Me-Up

Despite our best efforts and preparation, sometimes a lesson just doesn't go as planned. Help lift your student teacher's spirits when she hits a rough spot by giving her a small token of support. Keep on hand several inexpensive items, such as a candy bar or a package of sticky notes featuring a humorous message. When your student teacher has a less-than-perfect day, place one of these items on her desk as a morale booster.

Nancy Murphy—Gr. 5, Converse School, Beloit, WI

A Photographic Welcome

Acquaint your student teacher with your students long before she ever meets them with the help of a school yearbook. Send your student teacher a school yearbook with the names of students in your class highlighted. Or have each child write a letter of introduction to the student teacher; then attach a wallet-size photo of each child to his letter. Mail the letters to the student teacher. What a great way to give your student teacher a head start on remembering students' names and faces!

Patricia E. Dancho
Apollo-Ridge Middle School
Spring Church, PA

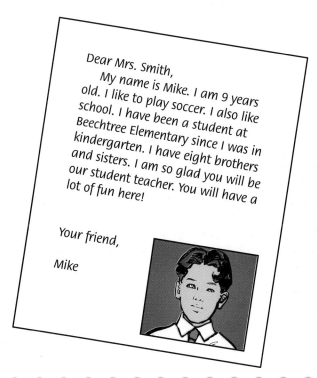

Dear Mrs. Smith,
My name is Mike. I am 9 years old. I like to play soccer. I also like school. I have been a student at Beechtree Elementary since I was in kindergarten. I have eight brothers and sisters. I am so glad you will be our student teacher. You will have a lot of fun here!

Your friend,

Mike

Student Teachers

Interactive Journal

A three-ring binder is all you need to provide your student teacher with important information and invaluable feedback. Fill a three-ring binder with useful information, such as schedules, school policies, and grade-level teaching objectives. Place stickers, awards, and sticky notes in the binder pockets; then put some paper in the rings. Record positive comments, questions, and suggestions on the pages during your student teacher's lesson. Have your student teacher respond on the page in the same way right after the lesson. What a great way to establish a productive dialogue!

Debbie Schneck—Gr. 4
Fogelsville Elementary, Schnecksville, PA

A Box of Great Ideas

As a veteran teacher, one of the most valuable things you can give your student teacher is the benefit of your years of classroom experience. Take advantage of that experience to create this handy, inexpensive going-away gift for your student teacher. Label several file card dividers with categories, such as five-minute fillers, bulletin boards, games, and arts-and-crafts activities. Then record your favorite ideas on index cards and file them behind the appropriate dividers. Give the file box to your student teacher on her last day with your class.

Susan Layne—Grs. K–5

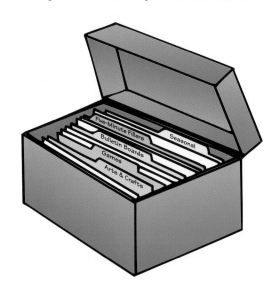

Daily Debriefing

Keep your student teacher informed of his progress by setting up a daily conference. On your schedule, allot ten to 20 minutes at the end of the day to meet with your student teacher. During the meeting, allow the student teacher to ask questions and make comments about his progress. Then discuss the day's lessons in terms of what went well and areas where improvements can be made. End the session by outlining goals for the following day. Your student teacher will appreciate being given this one-on-one time with you and will welcome the chance to get your valuable feedback.

Susan Keller—Gr. 5, Plumb Elementary, Largo, FL

File-Folder Fill-Up

Set your student teacher on the road toward success with this practical tip. Label a cardboard storage box "Student Teacher"; then place inside the box folders labeled with categories, such as five-minute fillers, discipline ideas, holiday/seasonal activities, bulletin boards, and patterns. Fill each folder with helpful ideas, activities, and information. Give this box of folders to your student teacher on her arrival and have her add to it daily. Encourage your student teacher to take the box with her when she leaves to use as a handy reference in her own classroom.

Janet Moody, J. W. Faulk Elementary, Lafayette, LA

Journal of Inspiration

Show your student teacher just how much he meant to your class with the following idea. Purchase an unlined journal with a decorative cover; then glue a photograph of each child on a separate page in the book. Next, have each student write a personal message to the student teacher on the page with her picture. Remind the student to mention the things she enjoyed about the student teacher's time in your class and to wish the student teacher well. The result will be a keepsake that will be an inspiration for your student teacher for years to come!

Brenda Shumake—Gr. 4, North Jackson Elementary, Jefferson, GA

Student Teacher Hope Chest

Send your student teacher off to her first job with a gift she'll love! Explain to students that they will be creating a hope chest for your student teacher as a going-away gift. Then send home a copy of one half of page 82 with each child. Ask each student to consult with his parents and select an item from the list to include in the chest. Place students' contributions in a plastic tub decorated with the student teacher's name along with the students' signatures. Present the hope chest to the student teacher at a shower, complete with cake and punch. Your student teacher will leave your classroom with lots of wonderful memories and a container of useful items to get her off to a great start in her own classroom!

Dr. Shirley Jacob, Southeastern Louisiana University Hammond, LA

Capture the Moment

Keep an annotated record of your student teacher's teaching experiences with the help of a disposable camera. Take photographs of day-to-day activities throughout the practicum. Then mount the photos in a scrapbook along with artwork and testimonials written by each student. Present the completed scrapbook at a farewell potluck luncheon in honor of your student teacher. Be sure to invite the student teacher's family to the luncheon to help you wish her the best of luck!

Deborah Abrams Burroughs—Gr. 5
Laguna Elementary
Laguna, NM

It's a Date!

Help your student teacher keep track of important dates by giving her a labeled wall calendar. Purchase an inexpensive wall calendar; then spend a few minutes recording dates of important school-related events on it. Include events such as holidays, in-service workshops, report card and progress report issue dates, teacher meetings, and field trips. Present the programmed calendar to your student teacher on her first day. Having this important information from the start will allow your student teacher to be prepared and make the most of her time with your class.

Patricia E. Dancho
Apollo-Ridge Middle School
Spring Church, PA

January

Sun.	Mon.	Tues.	Wed.	Thurs.	Fri.	Sat.
				1	2	3
4	5	6	7	8 Open house!	9	10
11	12 BAKE SALE!	13	14	15	16	17
18	19	20 Trip to Zoo! 2:00	21	22	23 PTA 7:00	24
25	26	27	28	29	30	31

Instant Activity File

It's a safe bet to say that almost every teacher has a file of favorite, tried-and-true activities. Help your student teacher start her own such file by placing one additional copy of each of your favorite activities in a file folder labeled "For the Student Teacher." Add an activity to the folder each time you place one in your own files. When you are assigned a student teacher, invite her to look through the file and select any activities that she would like to copy. Your student teacher will truly appreciate having her own personal collection of activities to take with her when she leaves.

Susan Layne—Grs. K–5, Otter River Elementary, Goode, VA

A Gift From the Heart...and Hands

Send warm wishes to your student teacher with this crafty going-away gift. Cut a 6" x 6" muslin square for each student in your class. On a day when your student teacher is observing in another classroom, have each student dip her hand in fabric paint and make an impression on her square. Next, have the student use a fabric marker to sign her name on the square. Sew the squares together in a quilt formation, or have a parent volunteer do this step. Add additional squares as needed to square off the design. Then sew a plain white sheet to the back of the quilted arrangement as a backing. Have students use dull-tipped needles and four-inch lengths of embroidery floss to tie off the quilt at the corner of each muslin square. Wrap the completed quilt in a large box and attach to it a copy of the poem on the right. Then present the gift to your student teacher at a farewell gathering.

Christine Smyth—Gr. 5, Frank Jewett Elementary, West Buxton, ME

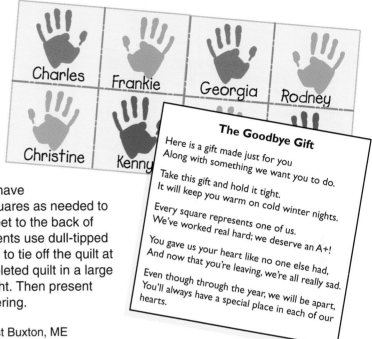

The Goodbye Gift

Here is a gift made just for you
Along with something we want you to do.

Take this gift and hold it tight.
It will keep you warm on cold winter nights.

Every square represents one of us.
We've worked real hard; we deserve an A+!

You gave us your heart like no one else had,
And now that you're leaving, we're all really sad.

Even though through the year, we will be apart,
You'll always have a special place in each of our hearts.

Student Teacher Appreciation Song

Create a musical tribute to your student teacher. First, have your students select a favorite song tune. Next, brainstorm together words that describe the experiences the class has enjoyed with the student teacher. Put the words to the music and practice the final piece. On the student teacher's last day, surprise her by singing the song and presenting her with a written copy.

Mary Dinneen, Mountain View School, Bristol, CT

Ring in Success

Equip your student teacher with the tools he needs for a successful experience with this practical idea. Purchase a three-ring binder and fill it with several section dividers. Label each divider with a heading like those listed below; then fill each section with related information:

- Class Information—class list, seating chart
- School Information—staff list, phone numbers and addresses, school discipline plan, cafeteria menu
- Schedules—class schedules, school-year calendar
- Forms—supply requisitions, attendance forms, discipline referrals, etc.
- Teaching Tips—teaching strategies, articles on teaching

Give your student teacher the binder on his first day; then encourage him to add important information to it throughout his student-teaching experience.

Sharon Caskey—Gr. 4, Lincoln Elementary, Marshfield, WI

Video Hail and Farewell

If a picture is worth a thousand words, then this video for your student teacher will be priceless! Use a video camera to have your students introduce themselves to a new student teacher or say goodbye to one who is leaving soon. Video-tape a short message from each of your students. Or, if you have a limited amount of time, take photographs of each child and have her write a personalized message to the student teacher. Mount the photos and accompanying messages in a decorated photo album. Also provide the student teacher with an inexpensive single-use camera for taking pictures of the class, bulletin boards, and projects before he leaves.

Patricia E. Dancho
Apollo-Ridge Middle School
Spring Church, PA

Autographs, Please!

This is one going-away gift that your student teacher is sure to go ape over! Purchase an autographable stuffed animal. Have each student sign her name on the stuffed animal using a permanent laundry marker. Present the autographed animal to your student teacher on her last day as a special reminder of her student-teaching experience.

Kelly A. Wong, Berlyn School, Ontario, CA

Thanks for the Memories

This inexpensive keepsake is sure to be treasured by your student teacher for years to come! Purchase a 4" x 6" photo album. Decorate the cover with an inspirational poem related to teaching. Glue additional copies of poems and inspiring thoughts to 4" x 6" cards, and place them in the album's photo-protector sheets. Then place a photograph of your class in the album along with several shots of your student teacher working with students. Fill the remaining album space with small notes and drawings from individual students. Present the album to your student teacher at a going-away party on her last day.

Beverly Langland
Trinity Christian Academy, Jacksonville, FL

Top It Off With a Tape

End your student teacher's experience on a high note with the help of a tape recorder and an audiocassette. Record each child telling the student teacher the special memories he has of their experience together. Give the tape to the student teacher and remind him to listen to it whenever he needs to lift his spirits.

Susan C. Russell—Grs. 3–4 Gifted and Talented
Susie E. Tolbert Elementary
Jacksonville, FL

First-Class Advice

Give your student teacher a first-class send-off with a little help from your students. Provide each student with an 8½" x 11" sheet of paper. Have him record on his paper a few words of advice for the student teacher to remember as she begins her teaching career. Allow students to come up with serious or humorous advice, such as "Always listen to your students" or "Never give homework." Then have each student illustrate his piece of advice and glue a small photo of himself to the back of the page. Staple the completed pages together and attach a cover titled "First-Class Advice."

Laura Labyak—Gr. 5, Western Branch Intermediate, Chesapeake, VA

We're All Thumbs!

Give your student teacher a going-away gift that's sure to get a thumbs-up from everyone! Purchase a plain canvas bag or an apron with pockets. Have each student dip his thumb into permanent ink and make a thumbprint on the gift; then have him use permanent markers to decorate the thumbprint to look like an animal character. Next, have the student sign his name below his thumbprint character. Once each student has had the chance to add to the tote bag, fill it with several popular book titles. Or, if you decorated an apron, fill it with school supplies. Present the decorative bag or apron to your student teacher as a farewell gift.

Debbie Schneck—Gr. 4
Fogelsville Elementary
Schnecksville, PA

Substitute Teachers

No Substitute for Preparation

As you prepare your substitute folder for the new year, be sure to include a special class pictorial. Duplicate your students' photos from last year's yearbook. Cut out each photo and paste it next to the student's name on a class chart. When it comes to acquainting a substitute with your students, what a difference a picture makes!

Pamela J. Fox—Gr. 4
Brassfield Elementary
Bixby, OK

Jackson Crane

Janet Anthony

Graham Bell

Substitute Plans

Each year I make a skeleton outline of my daily schedule. I keep a supply of copies both at school and at home. Whenever I need a substitute to take over my class, I simply fill out the form with my plans. This duplicated outline saves me from having to write out all of the details of my daily schedule every time I need a substitute.

Karen Womack—Gr. 4
Dardanelle Intermediate
Russellville, AR

Substitute Plans

Date:
Tues.:   Lunchroom duty
Fri.:   Morning & recess duty
8:05–8:10   Lockers
8:10–9:10   Period 1 (check roll, lunch count, supplies)

9:10–10:05 Math

Surprise Rewards

Want to ensure good student behavior while you're away at a conference or workshop? Then try this surprise reward plan. Choose small rewards for each day that you are going to be out of the classroom. Write the rewards on separate index cards. Fold and staple each card so that the reward cannot be seen. Post on your classroom calendar one card on each day that you are going to be absent. Explain to the students that at the end of each day, the substitute teacher will take the card off the calendar and give the students with good behavior the prize listed on the card. This system also works well the week before a holiday.

Julie Granchelli, Lockport, NY

Sticky Note Substitute Plans

One of the many difficulties for busy teachers is finding the time to write lesson plans that are clear and specific enough in the event of an unexpected absence. Daily plans often need to be rearranged, which makes matters worse! Help solve this problem by writing lesson plans for the week on Post-it Brand notes. Plans can be rearranged in your planbook as necessary and are ready at a moment's notice in case the need for a substitute should arise. Just think—you'll be able to concentrate on feeling better instead of worrying about having to rush to rewrite plans!

Melissa M. Jones—Gr. 4
Waynesville Elementary
Waynesville, OH

Reading
Read pages 25–32.

Complete discussion questions 1–5.

Math
1. Review fives times tables.
2. Play "Around the World."
3. Assign page 258 (1–4).

Substitute Icebreaker

Need a novel way to break the ice with the children for whom you are substituting? Provide each student with a sheet of lined paper, instructing him to fold it in half like a greeting card. On the front of the paper, have the student write three to five sentences about himself including information such as likes, dislikes, hobbies, and physical traits. The student should then write his name on the inside of his paper. Fill out one for yourself too. Collect the papers and share the information, allowing students time to guess who is being described on each card. Keep these on hand to fill in spare minutes throughout the day. Students will enjoy discovering how well they know their classmates and learning about you too!

Pamela Doerr—Substitute Teacher, Elizabethtown, PA

Time Fillers

Opening Routines

Before School

Supporting Your Substitute

Get your substitute teacher off to a great start with this helpful organizational tip. Use several 4" x 6" index cards to outline your classroom routines. Some sample card headings could include "Before School," "Opening Routines," "Time Fillers," "Emergency Procedures," and "End of the Day." On each of the cards, record the appropriate information about your classroom routines. Laminate the cards and bind them together with a metal ring. The cards save you time because you do not have to rewrite the same information each day you are absent. They are also an invaluable reference for your substitute.

Leslie Jackson—Substitute Teacher
Aschaffenburg Elementary
Aschaffenburg, Germany

On the Lookout for Helping Hands!

Extra pairs of hands—whether helping in the classroom or at home—are always appreciated. Please take a look at the list below and circle any volunteer opportunities in which you're interested. Then fill in the information requested at the bottom of this form and return it within two weeks. The students and I thank you for your help!

Please get involved!

Sincerely,

In the classroom...

 Reader: Reads aloud to the class.

 Field Trip Processor: Collects and counts field trip money; makes sure collected money balances with what is needed.

Book Order Processor: Tallies and processes book orders; makes sure collected money balances with what is needed.

 Writing Workshop Assistant: Helps with editing students' writing; gives feedback to students.

 Math Assistant: Helps students who need reinforcement of skills.

 Chaperone: Assists with field trips.

 Computer Assistant: Helps students with word processing.

At home...

Baker: Bakes items for classroom or unit parties.

 **Artist:** Creates artwork for bulletin boards, displays, etc.

Telephoner: Calls students/parents to relay teacher-created messages.

Audiotape Recorder: Tape-records selections provided by the teacher.

Room Parent: Helps organize classroom celebrations.

Signature _____

Telephone Number _____

Child's Name _____

Note to the teacher: See "Sign Up Here, Please!" on page 45. Make a photocopy of this page. Customize the copy by adding the approximate time commitment required after each job description. Add your signature below "Sincerely" before duplicating.

Resources Inventory

Title of unit: _____   **Subject:** _____

	title of resource	kind of resource	location
1.			
2.			
3.			
4.			
5.			
6.			
7.			
8.			
9.			
10.			

Contacts... *for field trips and guest speakers:*

	name	address	phone number
1.			
2.			
3.			

Note to the teacher: See "Unit Resources at Your Fingertips" on page 52 for information on how to use this reproducible form.

A B C
1 2 3

_____

Dear Parent,

On _____ our class will be hosting a new teacher shower for our student teacher. If you would like to contribute an item for the hope chest we are putting together, please consider any one of the following items. Please have your child bring your item to school by _____.

Thank you,

_____

New Teacher Gift Registry

- file folders
- index cards
- postage stamps
- paper
- pens
- pencils
- stapler
- staples
- paper clips
- three-ring binder
- construction paper
- scissors
- nametags
- felt-tipped pens

- Band-Aid bandages
- plastic storage containers
- tissues
- three-hole puncher
- ruler
- stencils
- rubber bands
- clear tape
- masking tape
- clear Con-Tact paper
- desk calendar
- wall calendar
- minute timer
- hand lotion

- chalk
- transparency markers
- two-sided tape
- staple remover
- sticky notes
- baby wipes
- plastic bags
- reward stickers
- rubber stamps
- brads
- cotton swabs
- spray bottle
- glue stick
- breath mints

To My Student Teacher

A B C D E F V W X Y Z

A B C D E F G H I J K L M N O P Q R S T U V W X Y Z

A B C
1 2 3

_____

Dear Parent,

On _____ our class will be hosting a new teacher shower for our student teacher. If you would like to contribute an item for the hope chest we are putting together, please consider any one of the following items. Please have your child bring your item to school by _____.

Thank you,

_____

New Teacher Gift Registry

- file folders
- index cards
- postage stamps
- paper
- pens
- pencils
- stapler
- staples
- paper clips
- three-ring binder
- construction paper
- scissors
- nametags
- felt-tipped pens

- Band-Aid bandages
- plastic storage containers
- tissues
- three-hole puncher
- ruler
- stencils
- rubber bands
- clear tape
- masking tape
- clear Con-Tact paper
- desk calendar
- wall calendar
- minute timer
- hand lotion

- chalk
- transparency markers
- two-sided tape
- staple remover
- sticky notes
- baby wipes
- plastic bags
- reward stickers
- rubber stamps
- brads
- cotton swabs
- spray bottle
- glue stick
- breath mints

To My Student Teacher

©The Education Center, Inc. • *500 Classroom Tips* • TEC60849

A B C D E F V W X Y Z

Note to the teacher: Use with "Student Teacher Hope Chest" on page 73.

Contents

Assessment

Assessment Calendars

Assessment is an ongoing part of my daily routine. One helpful tool that I use is a blank monthly calendar for each student. I store the calendars on a clipboard that I keep with me throughout the day. During group work or individual conferences, I jot down notes and comments for that day on the calendars. At the end of the month, I file the calendars and clip new copies to my clipboard. When it's time for parent conferences, I share my observations of each child. Now I don't have to rely so much on my memory!

Katie Kasar—Gr. 4, Carollton Elementary
Oak Creek, WI

How Did Group Time Go Today?

Having a large class, I found it difficult to monitor group dynamics and progress on the skills involved in cooperative learning. Since I can't become a "fly on the wall," I devised an evaluation sheet that each student completes after working with his/her group. On the sheet, the student rates his performance as well as that of his teammates. Students are encouraged to provide specific comments about what transpired during group time (knowing that all comments will be strictly confidential). These evaluation sheets keep me informed about the progress students are making on their social skills and help me understand what might be causing a lack of progress. Plus the insights on group dynamics gained by having students complete these evaluations help me hold productive group conferences.

Barbara E. Peek, Andalusia, AL

Rubric Sheet Suggestions

Whenever I assign a class project, I provide each student with a rubric sheet to use as a checklist. On the sheet, I include space for parents to jot down their comments and suggestions for the project. I award bonus points to each student who returns his checklist signed by a parent.

Patricia E. Dancho, Apollo-Ridge Middle School
Spring Church, PA

Bimonthly Progress Report

Part of my portfolio assessment program includes bimonthly progress reports. Every two weeks I complete a progress report that evaluates a student's work during that time period. I discuss the report privately with the child. If the student and I identify any specific areas to improve, I have him reflect on ways to improve the problem area; then I have him note his ideas for improvement on the progress report. A copy of the finished report is placed in the child's portfolio; another copy is mailed to his parents. These individual conferences and progress reports allow me to identify my students' opinions about their work and correct any misconceptions about expectations, assignment objectives, and learning goals.

Werna R. Pierce, Myrtle Beach, SC

A — **A**wesome	**N** — **N**eat
B — **B**e Proud	**O** — **O**utstanding
C — **C**lever Writing	**P** — **P**erfect or **P**ractically Perfect
D — **D**ynamite Work	**Q** — **Q**uite Good
E — **E**xcellent Effort	**R** — **R**ight On
F — **F**antastic	**S** — **S**uperior
G — **G**ood Going	**T** — **T**otally Great
H — **H**ow Wonderful	**U** — **U**nbelievable
I — **I** Like This	**V** — **V**ery Good
J — **J**ust Super	**W** — **W**ow
K — **K**ing-Size Work	**X** — **X**-cellent
L — **L**ove It	**Y** — **Y**ou've Got It
M — **M**ighty Effort	**Z** — **Z**ounds

The ABCs of Positive Comments

Writing positive comments on a student's paper is important in building self-esteem. A problem I face, however, is using and reusing the same comments again and again. So I devised an alphabetical list of words and phrases to take the sameness out of grading. Use this list, or substitute words and phrases of your own.

Sandra Lowery—Gr. 4
Leavenworth, KS

For the Record

Anecdotal records are a valuable resource for teachers during conferences and around report card time. Make keeping these records a simpler task with the help of adhesive file-folder labels. Keep a sheet of labels on your clipboard and carry it with you at all times. When you feel the need to document a student's behavior, write the child's name, the date, and a brief summary on one of the labels. Later, adhere the label inside the student's folder. Individualized record keeping was never easier!

Stephany R. Ezekiel—Gr. 4, Scotland Elementary, Scotland, AK

Assessment

It's in the Cards!

Checking every single homework paper would be fine *if* you didn't have a life outside the classroom! Curtail the paper chase with this simple idea. Give each child a laminated paper square, with one side colored red and the other side green. Write the answer to the first homework problem on the chalkboard. If a student agrees with the answer, he holds up his card so that the green side is showing. If he disagrees, he holds up the red side. At a glance, I pinpoint any child who is having a problem with a particular concept; then I pair him with a classmate who answered the problem correctly so that they can find his error and correct it. With this method, students get immediate attention, without having to wait a day or more to receive a corrected paper. My students love this speedy way of checking work. And I love the fact that my desk isn't covered with homework papers to grade!

Carol Irvine—Grs. 4–5, West End School, North Plainfield, NJ

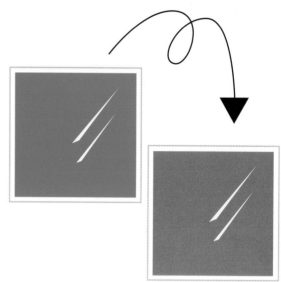

Creative-Writing Portfolios

A great place to start using portfolios is with your writing program. Each of my students uses crayons or markers to personalize a two-pocket folder. Assessments are stored in one side of the folder and work samples in the other. After a specific time period, such as grading period, I give each child a reaction sheet similar to the one on page 107. Students, parents, and teacher evaluate the work samples and complete the reaction sheet. Reaction sheets are kept in the assessment pocket until the end of the year. During the last month of school, we hold a Portfolio Party to celebrate my students' writing progress. Each child orally shares his favorite published work, an assignment that was the most challenging, his most humorous work, etc. It's a super way to end our portfolio assessment adventure!

Sandra Preston—Gr. 5, Albany School of Humanities, Albany, NY

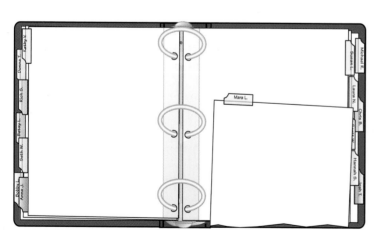

Information Superbook

Keep all of your students' vital information in one place with this super simple idea. Purchase a large three-ring binder and add a tabbed divider for each student. Store in the notebook for each child important information, such as goals determined by parents, the student, and the teacher; work samples for each grading period; concerns that a parent or a student has that you need to be aware of; reading records; assessments; and parent communications. Remove and send home items periodically, or keep everything until the end of the year. Either way, you'll have a handy, organized record of each student's progress and parent communications.

Donna Viola—Grs. 4/5, Roosevelt Elementary
McPherson, KS

Rubric Labels

Who says assessing your students' writing pieces has to take a long time? It doesn't anymore with this idea. Use a word processing program to create and print a rubric label such as the one shown. When students turn in their final copies, stick a label on each paper. Then circle a number in each row to indicate your assessment of that area (with 1 indicating mastery and 5 indicating a need for remediation). In just moments, students will be able to read your informal assessment and know how they did on the assignment. Extend this idea by creating additional rubrics for other subject areas.

Anita M. Nixon, Frank J. Dugan Elementary
Marlboro, NJ

Capitalization	1 2 3 4 5
Punctuation	1 2 3 4 5
Spelling	1 2 3 4 5
Complete sentences	1 2 3 4 5
Indent new paragraph	1 2 3 4 5
Paragraph skills	1 2 3 4 5
Neatness	1 2 3 4 5

Student Conferences

Holding frequent student conferences may be time-consuming, but it's time well spent if you want to raise responsible students. Twice a quarter, I meet privately with each child to discuss his or her progress. We discuss questions such as the following:
- Do you think you are doing your best? Why or why not?
- In what areas are you making the most progress? In what areas would you like to improve?
- What do you plan to do to help yourself make even more progress? What can I do to help you progress?
- What suggestions do you have about how I could be a better teacher?

Discussing these questions reminds students that, though I'm there to help in any way I can, their schoolwork is their responsibility.

Debra Lynn Neal—Gr. 4, Bay Area Christian Academy, Sandusky, OH

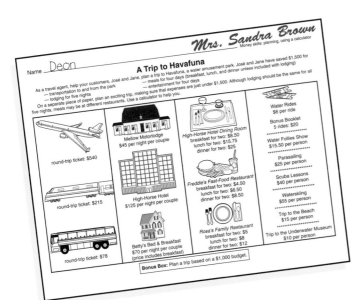

When Parents Help

Just because a student makes 100 percent on a homework assignment doesn't necessarily mean that she understood a concept. At the beginning of the year, ask parents to sign the top of any homework assignment they needed to help their children with. If a parent's signature is across the top of an assignment, it will signal to you that the student needs extra help on that skill.

Joan Cuba—Gr. 5
Pleviak School
Lake Villa, IL

Anecdotal Notes at Your Fingertips

With more emphasis on accountability, organizing and keeping daily information on each child has become even more important. I've found the following technique to be quite effective. Place a 5" x 8" lined index card near the bottom edge of an open folder. Tape the card in place as shown. Place a second card on top of the first one, matching its top edge to the top line of the first card. Tape the second card in place. Continue adding a card for each child, using both sides of the open folder. Label each card with a student's name. All of the cards are now at your fingertips for recording those important anecdotal notes. These index cards hold a lot of information, and the final product is both inexpensive and easy to make.

Reba S. Walden—Chapter I Reading
Granite Falls Elementary, Granite Falls, NC

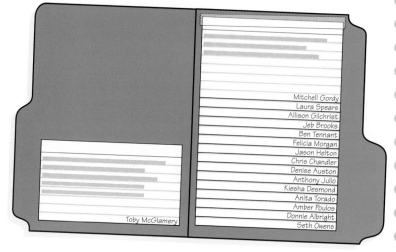

A Simple System

If you're eager to get started with portfolios, try this idea. Have each student file all of his graded work in a "Work Samples" folder. Near the end of each grading period, have students select a predetermined number of samples from each subject area to place in their portfolios. Select a few samples yourself, marking the top of each with a *T*. Attach to the work samples a duplicated student self-evaluation form that includes space for teacher and parent comments. Have students take the portfolios and self-evaluations home to share with parents and return them to file for future reference. This system is a super way to introduce portfolios to both students and teachers.

adapted from an idea by Suzanne Whitehurst—Gr. 5, Lake Magdalene Elementary, Tampa, FL

STUDENT	M	T	W	T	F
Toby	93	100	0		
Sue	78	46	76		
Angie	83	91	95		
Nick	61	83	84		
Zachary	94	85	97		
Cayce	58	89	90		

Sept. 13–17

Colorful Grades

Cut down on the time spent averaging grades with this simple tip. When you enter grades into your gradebook, write passing grades in blue ink and failing grades in red. At a glance you can quickly scan to see who needs a progress report or parent conference. To save even more time, highlight the column for each quiz you give. Then when you need to average test scores, you won't have to search through all your grades to locate them.

Julie Kwoka—Gr. 5
George Southard Elementary
Lockport, NY

Writing Checklists

Both students and teachers sometimes find it difficult to evaluate writing. I describe the components of the writing piece we're currently working on and create a checklist for students to use as they write. I model the components emphasized on the checklist, usually on the overhead projector. Then the students work together to create some models on their own before starting on their individual pieces. Checklists take the mystery out of the grading process and help me focus more on the goals I want students to achieve. Parents especially prefer this outline format over a general grade.

Mary Gates—Gr. 4, Huckleberry Hill School, Brookfield, CT

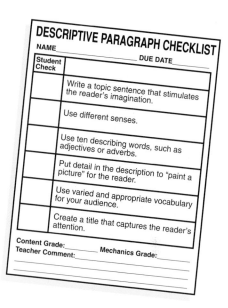

DESCRIPTIVE PARAGRAPH CHECKLIST

NAME _____
DUE DATE _____

Student Check	
	Write a topic sentence that stimulates the reader's imagination.
	Use different senses.
	Use ten describing words, such as adjectives or adverbs.
	Put detail in the description to "paint a picture" for the reader.
	Use varied and appropriate vocabulary for your audience.
	Create a title that captures the reader's attention.

Content Grade:_____ Mechanics Grade:_____
Teacher Comment:_____

Portfolio Notebooks

At the beginning of the school year, I ask each student to purchase a three-ring binder notebook with divider tabs. We label the tabs to make sections such as "Writer's Workshop," "Response to Reading," "English Skills," and "Miscellaneous." All student work is dated; then it is hole-punched and placed in the binders. Notes taken during individual reading and writing conferences are also stored in the binders.

At the end of the first quarter, each student selects a few items from each section to place in his portfolio. Students reflect on their chosen samples and complete various evaluation forms before taking the portfolios home to share with parents. Then they return the portfolios to school. At the end of the second quarter, each child removes some work samples from the portfolio and adds new pieces to show progress in each subject area. Not only is this system easy to manage, it also results in an end-of-the-year portfolio that shows a child's progress over the entire year.

Janyce Ostrander—Gr. 5, Rousseau Elementary, Lincoln, NE

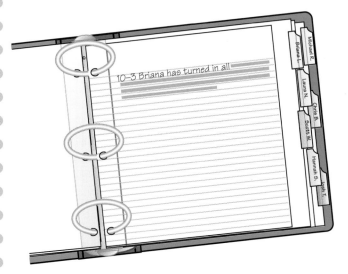

10–3 Briana has turned in all

How Well Do You Know Your Students?

I keep a binder notebook with a labeled section for each student with me at all times. I use this notebook to keep track of each child's accomplishments, behavior, funny sayings, special moments, etc. My notebook not only provides invaluable documentation for evaluation purposes, it also is a wonderful tool for parent-teacher conferences. Single clues about a child can often be missed. But when I see all of the clues together on one page, it's easier for me to recognize patterns or problems. I'm careful to date all entries as well as record the source of my information (observed by me, reported by another teacher or student, etc.). My notebook is a teaching tool that I wouldn't want to be without!

Kathleen Jordan, Orange County Schools
Altamonte Springs, FL

Assessment

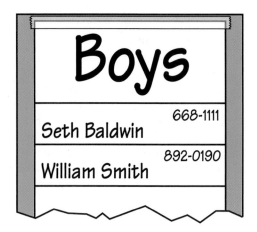

Easy Anecdotal Records

You'll flip over this easy way to keep track of students' behavior! Cut a 12" x 18" piece of poster board. Starting at the bottom of the poster board, stack index cards as shown. Then tape each card at the top. Finally, write a student's name and phone number at the bottom of each card. Simply flip to a student's card to document phone calls, concerns, improvements, etc. Make a separate chart for boys and for girls; or make a smaller chart for each of your co-operative groups.

Cheryl Radley—Grs. 3–4, Lake Norman Elementary, Mooresville, NC

Report Card Relief

Don't be left hanging during report card time! Put a labeled hanging file folder for each student in one of your desk or filing-cabinet drawers. Use the folders to store notes on student behavior, work samples, classroom observations, and other valuable documentation. When you are ready to begin working on report cards, take home a few student files at a time and use the helpful information to complete the evaluations in no time at all. These folders also serve as a great reference at conference time!

Wendy Bousquet—Substitute Grs. K–6, Scarborough, Ontario, Canada

Work Samples Organizer

Collecting work samples so that students have a ready supply from which to choose portfolio components can be a management challenge. To collect samples to place in our writing portfolios, I label an expandable file for each student. Inside each file I place dividers (made by cutting apart colored file folders). The dividers are labeled with categories such as "Personal Narrative," "Poetry," "Prose," "Content Areas," etc. My students can easily file their writing samples inside the files. Plus they no longer must flip through every sample when searching for a particular type of writing.

Karen Alford—Gr. 4, Rich Pond Elementary
Bowling Green, KY

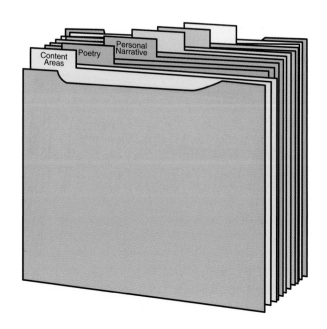

QUESTIONNAIRE

1. Did you mispronounce words?
   Frequently   Sometimes   Never
2. Did you skip words?
   Frequently   Sometimes   Never
3. Did you pause in the middle of sentences?
   Frequently   Sometimes   Never
4. Did you use good expression?
   Frequently   Sometimes   Never
5. Did you understand the story as you read?
   Frequently   Sometimes   Never
6. What did you learn about your reading today?
   _____
   _____

Do I Sound Like That?

Self-assessment is a powerful tool that has opened many of my students' eyes. I tape-record each student as he reads for 30 seconds or several paragraphs. The student must note the material he read so that he can easily locate it later. I tape about five students on one audiocassette, noting the order on the outside of the cassette. During a quiet, whole-class activity, each student listens to himself on a Walkman tape player as he follows along in the book. As a student listens, he fills out a questionnaire like the one shown. Then that child passes the tape player and tape to the next person listed on that cassette.

Lauri Wedel-Isaacs—Gr. 4, L'Ouverture Magnet School
Wichita, KS

Self-Evaluation Reports

When evaluating I often find that my best resources are the students themselves. I have each child keep a portfolio of his work in a classroom folder. At the end of each quarter, I distribute the folders and have the students organize their work. Students are then asked to reflect on their work of the last quarter and set goals for the next quarter. I guide them through this process by distributing copies of a self-evaluation form (see page 109). I always review this self-evaluation form with parents at the beginning of a conference.

Loraine Moore—Gr. 4, Pearl Prep, El Monte, CA

Student Self-Evaluations

When I talk to my class about responsibility, I suggest that success comes from six key elements: focus, participation, good work habits, a positive attitude, independent skills, and citizenship. To reinforce these elements every day, I give each student a copy of a weekly self-evaluation chart (see page 108). At the end of the day, students evaluate themselves by completing their charts. Each student who has a "yes" in each column receives a puzzle piece. When the student has earned 20 pieces, he assembles his puzzle, which is actually a free homework certificate that I've cut into 20 pieces. (You can also reward students with special coupons from area businesses, such as a miniature golf park or pizzeria.) With this system of self-evaluation, students think about their behavior and take ownership of it.

N. Jane Bond—Gr. 5, St. Augustine Country Day School
St. Augustine, FL

Name _____

Was I on Target Today?

Self-evaluation

How responsible were you today? Think about the behaviors and attitudes you exhibited. Write "yes" or "no" in each box.

	MON.	TUES.	WED.	THURS.	FRI.
FOCUS Did I concentrate and pay attention?					
PARTICIPATION Did I contribute in class and/or in my group?	yes	yes			
GOOD WORK HABITS Did I put forth my best effort?	yes	yes			
POSITIVE ATTITUDE Did I believe in myself?	yes	yes			
INDEPENDENT SKILLS When working alone, did I use my time wisely?	yes	yes			
CITIZENSHIP Did I _____	yes	yes			

Education Center, Inc. • 500 Classroom Tips • TEC60849

Yahoo!
Take a homework break
(Good for one free homework assignment)

Assessment

Learning Logs

To help my students become independent learners and develop self-evaluation skills, I have each child make a learning log. To make a log, each student staples paper inside a folder. Each week students select samples of completed work to put in manila envelopes. They also write in their learning logs, explaining to parents what they're learning and what they need to work on. Instead of reporting only about their grades, I encourage students to answer questions such as

What did you learn this week?
What did you learn that was important?
How did you learn something this week?

What do you need to practice?
What do you need assistance with?
What did you accomplish that makes you feel good?

Students take their logs and envelopes home each Friday. On Monday I read each log to see if there are any parent concerns. Through learning logs, students, parents, and I have immediate feedback about how students are doing.

Brenda W. Myers, Bainbridge-Guilford Central School District, Bainbridge, NY

Trina's Learning Log

Count Their Corrections

Help your students learn from their mistakes with this Grade A tip! Begin by asking each student to find and circle her errors on a recently graded math test. Have the student explain her mistakes in writing; then have her detail the correct process or missed fact and redo the problem correctly. Grade and score the test again and average the two scores together for the final grade. Now you'll see a score that represents *true* learning!

Jane Mills—Gr. 5, Norman Rockwell School, Redmond, WA

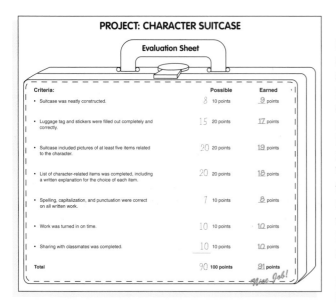

PROJECT: CHARACTER SUITCASE

Evaluation Sheet

Criteria:	Possible	Earned
• Suitcase was neatly constructed.	8 10 points	9 points
• Luggage tag and stickers were filled out completely and correctly.	15 20 points	17 points
• Suitcase included pictures of at least five items related to the character.	20 20 points	19 points
• List of character-related items was completed, including a written explanation for the choice of each item.	20 20 points	18 points
• Spelling, capitalization, and punctuation were correct on all written work.	7 10 points	8 points
• Work was turned in on time.	10 10 points	10 points
• Sharing with classmates was completed.	10 10 points	10 points
Total	90 100 points	91 points

Nice Job!

Students as Self-Evaluators

To help students become effective self-evaluators, I have them rate their projects before I grade them. When a project (such as a book report) is assigned, I give students the criteria that I will use to grade it. When the project is finished, each child rates her work on a copy of my evaluation sheet, adding anything that she wants me to know about her efforts to the bottom of her sheet. I grade the project on the same form the students use. Each child can then compare my opinions with hers. While my grade is the one recorded, I consider students' thoughts about their efforts, especially their written comments. Over time students develop a more critical eye when completing and evaluating projects. They also gain important insight about the qualities teachers look for in a finished project.

Phyllis Ellett—Grs. 3–4 Multiage, Earl Hanson Elementary Rock Island, IL

Assessment Notes

A grid of 2" x 1½" boxes—one box for each student—and two-inch Post-it brand notes help me organize my assessment comments. Each week I select a subject on which to observe students. During this time I make positive observations of several students on Post-it notes. I place each note over that child's name on the grid, which I keep on a clipboard. When I observe during that subject again the next day, I can easily see which students I still need to write comments on. At the end of the week, when the grid is full, I transfer all of the notes to a binder that has a page for each child. At the end of the grading period, I can easily transfer each binder page to a student's portfolio or attach it to his report card.

Cindy Hamilton—Gr. 5
Baldwin Intermediate School
Quincy, IL

Margo really participated in our problem-solving discussion.	Sid
Todd needs additional help with his multiplication facts.	Amber asked several questions about the homework assignment.

Makeup Grading

Eliminate the need to search for answer keys when grading makeup work with this easy tip! Make an extra copy of each test and reproducible your students complete. Label the top of each extra copy "Key" in bright red letters. Then use the red pen to fill in the answers. During the grading period, clip each key to the back of your gradebook or place it in a folder labeled "Keys." When students turn in makeup work, the answer keys will be handy and grading will be done in a flash!

Darby Herlong, Lugoff-Elgin Middle School, Lugoff, SC

January
Jonathan

M	T	W	Th	F
			1 Holiday! School's out!	**2** On task all day long!
5 Complained of headache most of the day.	**6** Helped Samantha with her multiplication tables.	**7** Forgot homework today.	**8** Art teacher praised behavior.	**9** Note from Mom: minor crisis at home.

Individualized Record Keeping

Looking for a quick and easy method to record observations of your students? At the beginning of each month, I program the dates on a blank calendar page, make a copy for each child, and hole-punch the pages to store in a binder. Then, each day as it's convenient, I record an entry on each student's calendar. At conference time, I share the calendars with parents. Parents always express appreciation for the individual attention that each child receives. In addition, the calendar often reveals a student's behavioral patterns.

Beth Pratt—Grs. 5 & 6 Multiage, Eastwood School, Sturgis, MI

Assessment

I think I deserve an A because

Anonymously Yours

At the end of each nine-week grading period, I invite my students to write anonymous letters to me. Each student must focus on three topics: the positive, the negative, and suggestions for the upcoming grading period. For each negative that a student includes, she must also write a positive comment or suggestion. As I read the letters, I highlight recurring topics such as too much homework, more homework exemptions, etc. It's often a real wake-up call for me! Sometimes I haven't been aware of some of the things students write about.

I also have each student write the grade she feels she deserves for the nine weeks on another sheet of paper. The student must also explain why she deserves that grade. It's always interesting to see how a student's perception of her progress aligns with mine! I keep these papers on file to share with parents during conferences.

Patricia Dancho, Apollo-Ridge Middle School, Spring Church, PA

Self-Checking Solution

After each student selects his answers on a multiple-choice or true/false assignment, have him color over his selections with a pink, a yellow, or an orange crayon. Then review the correct answers and have each student check his paper. With this easy suggestion, you won't have to worry about students being tempted to change incorrect answers (since they won't be able to erase over waxy crayon).

Wendy New—Gr. 5, Fairfield South Elementary, Cincinnati, OH

Grading My Project

Want students to take more ownership of the projects you assign? Then let them help create the assessment tool you'll use to grade them. Just follow these simple steps:

1. Draw a chart on the board as shown.
2. With students, discuss and determine the most important parts of the project (see the example). List their responses on the chart.
3. Work with students to determine the importance of each part. Then have students help designate a point value for each part as shown.
4. Type the completed grading chart and give a copy to each student. Direct students to use the chart as a guide for completing the project. Use the chart yourself as the project evaluation sheet.

Kelley Tijero
Creighton Intermediate School
Conroe, TX

Part	Points
island—drawn correctly; as large as possible	10
landforms—include 15 different ones on map; all labeled	30
paragraph—neatly written; describes origin of island	25
flag—colorful; includes paragraph describing symbols	20
followed all directions	15
TOTAL	100

Thumbs-Up, Thumbs-Down!

To quickly assess my class's understanding of a concept or agreement with an idea, I provide each student with two laminated cards, one labeled "Thumbs-Up" and the other "Thumbs-Down." These cards are very helpful during classroom debates and discussions. Instead of raising her hand, a student holds up one of her cards to show her feelings about an issue. Students share their opinions more independently because they don't know their classmates' responses.

Fran Abbagnaro—Gr. 5
Crockett School
Brentwood, TN

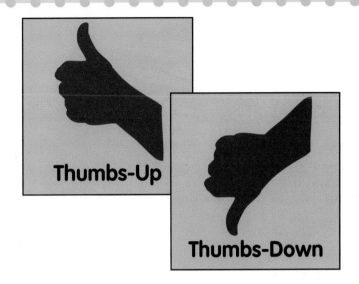
Thumbs-Up
Thumbs-Down

Report Card Tip

To help your students understand their educational progress, insert a personal note in the envelope with each child's report card. Be sure to include comments on their strengths as well as the areas that need improvement. This personal touch goes a long way toward helping students understand and feel good about their progress.

Ana L. Wilson, Ames School, Riverside, IL

Test Feedback
What grade did you earn?

Test Feedback Forms

My students are learning to process their study skills, analyze tests, and write in complete sentences. How? I attach a test feedback form to each major test that I give. On the form I ask the student to write the grade she thinks she's earned on the test, give reasons for her choice, and explain why she thought the test was difficult or easy. If the student answers all the questions on the form, she earns bonus points. However, if she doesn't respond in complete sentences or give reasons for her answers, only partial credit is given. My test feedback form has been an excellent motivational tool. Students now process what they've done. And I can note who has recognized effective—as well as ineffective—study skills.

Gail Hooker—Reading Fleming Middle School, Flemington, NJ

Departmentalized Teaching

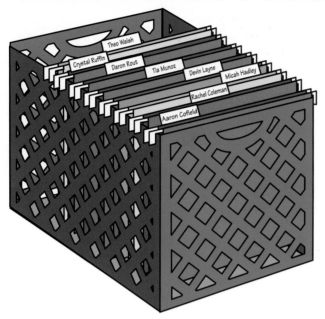

Organizing Graded Papers

When your kids change classes, getting graded papers filed and sent home can be an organizational challenge. To avoid a frustrating paper chase, purchase an inexpensive plastic crate for each homeroom class. Place a hanging file folder in the crate for each student. Then file graded papers inside the folders. When a second teacher wants to file her papers in your homeroom students' folders, just send her the crate.

Sharon Longton and Lisa Edwards—Gr. 4
Stovall Academy
Houston, TX

Once Upon a New Class...

Here's another no-fuss way to settle down your students after they've entered your room. After everyone has been seated, start the new class by reading aloud from a favorite children's novel for several minutes. This simple technique not only calms the class, but it also motivates reading and introduces students to some great literature.

Susan Keller and Jackie Fort—Gr. 5
Plumb Elementary
Clearwater, FL

Four Corners

When a new class enters your room, make sure supplies come with them with this idea. After everyone is seated, call out "Four corners!" Then have each student place his folder on the top left corner of his desk, his textbook on the top right corner, his pencil in the bottom right, and his homework in the bottom left. Scan the room to see who is prepared. In just a few short weeks, students will automatically remember this "four corners" reminder and bring their materials to class.

Mary Skelly
Salem Central School
Salem, NY

Returning Student Papers

Here's a hassle-free way to return graded papers to students who have several different teachers. Require that each student write the initial of his homeroom teacher's last name at the top of each assignment and then circle the letter. If you have more than one teacher in your group with the same initial, ask students to include the second (or an additional) letter of the name as well. In just a glance, you'll know where to send graded papers for filing or sending home.

Donna Viola—Grs. 4–5
McPherson, KS

Teachers on the Move

If having students change classes doesn't seem to be working, why not do the switching instead of your kids? When it's time to change classes, have the teachers swap classrooms, leaving the students ready to get to work at their own desks. Use a rolling cart to transport teacher's manuals and materials back and forth with ease. This simple solution translates into calmer students who aren't tempted to bother someone else's desk and personal supplies.

Jane Hutchison—Gr. 4, Tom Joy Elementary, Nashville, TN

Wipe-Off Organizers

With this handy tip, you and the other teachers on your team may never hear "What do I need today?" again! Hang a small dry-erase board outside each classroom. In the morning, have each teacher list the items students will need to bring with them to her class that day. So that students don't congregate around the board before class, also write the list on the board inside the classroom.

Michelle Zakula
St. Roman Catholic School
Milwaukee, WI

Today you will need:

• proposal for science fair project
• permission slip for Dec. 2 field trip
• pencil
• science journal

Departmentalized Teaching

Today you will need:
- Last night's homework
- Number cards
- Calculator
- Pencil
- Scrap paper

Materials Needed

With this easy-to-do tip, you won't waste another minute of valuable teaching time answering "What do we need today?" Before your new class arrives, list on the board the materials needed for that period. When students sit down, they'll know exactly what items to get out. Plus you'll be helping students learn important organizational skills.

Susan Keller and Jackie Fort—Gr. 5
Plumb Elementary
Clearwater, FL

Supplies Reminder Card

Students who travel between classrooms seem bound to forget something different every day. To save the time spent retrieving supplies, give each student a copy of a supplies card. On the card, list the supplies that students coming to your class will need. Laminate the cards; then have each child tape a copy onto his notebook. The only things students will leave behind now are their forgetful habits!

Marcia Worth-Baker, Gould School, North Caldwell, NJ

Listen Up!

Settle down students who are lined up to switch classes with this fun activity. Say the chant shown, with students repeating each line after you. When you get to the fourth line, announce a category related to a topic being studied, such as nouns, state capitals, multiplication facts, etc. When you get to the last line, announce the name of a student. Then have that child name an item in the stated category. In turn, each classmate standing in line with him must name a different item with no repeats. Great listening practice, plus a terrific way to review!

Mary Skelly
Salem Central School
Salem, NY

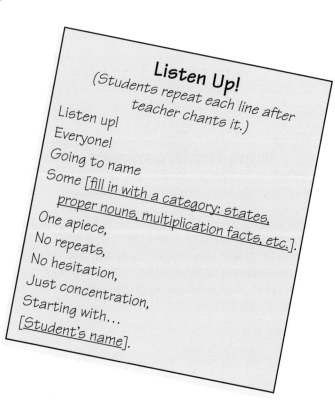

Listen Up!
(Students repeat each line after teacher chants it.)
Listen up!
Everyone!
Going to name
Some [fill in with a category: states, proper nouns, multiplication facts, etc.].
One apiece,
No repeats,
No hesitation,
Just concentration,
Starting with...
[Student's name].

Departmentalized Teaching

Kara

Class-Change Organizer

Students who travel between classrooms seem bound to forget materials from time to time. Solve this problem by supplying each child with a sturdy three- to four-inch-deep plastic pan that fits inside a desk. Have students fill their pans with class essentials and then carry the pans with them from class to class. Reuse the containers each year. The benefits? Neater desks, no complaints about materials being tampered with by others, and students who are more organized and responsible!

Debra Kiley—Gr. 5, Sandymount Elementary, Finksburg, MD

Community Calendar

It's every kid's (and parent's) worst nightmare: two tests or projects scheduled on the same date. Sidestep this hazard of changing classes with a simple solution. Each month post a large calendar outside your students' classrooms. Have each teacher use a different color of marker to label the calendar with all tests and projects due in her class that month. With this tip, teachers can avoid assigning multiple tests and projects on the same dates. The calendar will also help students and visiting parents keep up-to-date as well.

Michelle Zakula, St. Roman Catholic School, Milwaukee, WI

Road to Success

Send your students on a road trip that leads to responsible behavior with this cool contest. Use chalk to draw a dotted line down the middle of several sheets of black construction paper. Then mount the papers on a wall, as shown, to resemble a road. Using the chalk, mark at least 30 "miles" on the road as shown. Next, create a car template like the pattern shown. Label one cutout car for each of your classes.

When the display is ready, announce to students that each class will try to earn miles so that its car can travel down the Road to Success. Classes can earn up to five miles a day for each of the following:

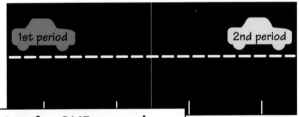

- Everyone enters and exits the room quietly.
- Everyone has all needed materials for class.
- Everyone completed the homework assignment.
- Everyone is seated and ready by [designate the time].
- The teacher doesn't have to stop teaching to address poor behavior.

At the end of the grading period, recognize the class whose car traveled the farthest with a reward of the students' choice (see the suggested list).

Sue Calaway—Gr. 5
Jack Hayes School, Monroe, LA

Vote for ONE reward:
- Extra five minutes of recess
- No-homework pass for each student
- Soda pop party
- Cookie party
- Ice-cream-sundae party
- Popcorn party
- Movie party
- Pizza party at lunch (students bring money)

Group Work

Pick a Partner

Forming cooperative groups is a cinch with this simple idea. All you need is a set of index cards.

- For pairs, program pairs of cards with synonyms, antonyms, homophones, states and capitals, or number-sentence parts (such as "5 x 6 =" and "30").
- For groups, program sets of index cards (four cards for forming groups of four, five for groups of five, etc.) with such items as geometric shapes, foods in the food groups from the Food Guide Pyramid, and colors.

Laminate the cards and store each set in a labeled Ziploc bag. To change groups or partners, place a set of cards in a container and shake it well. Then have each child draw a card and find its mate(s). If you have an odd number of students, add a "Free Choice" card to each batch, which allows its holder to work with the pair or group of his choice.

Carol Unanski—Gr. 4, Indian Hill Elementary, Holmdel, NJ

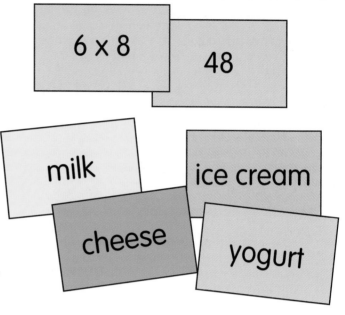

What a Deal!

Shuffle students into cooperative groups by using a deck of cards! Divide the deck into groups of four (four aces, four 8s, etc.) so that you have one card per child. Shuffle the cards; then give one to each student. Instruct him to find his three groupmates according to the number/picture on his card. Then assign a job to each student based on his card's suit: spades—reader, diamonds—group leader, hearts—recorder, and clubs—timekeeper. With this method, groups and jobs can be changed easily. What a deal!

Kristi Gettelman—Gr. 5, St. Roman Grade School, Milwaukee, WI

Forming Cooperative Groups

Looking for a new way to create cooperative groups? Stamp the backs of a supply of index cards (one per student) with four or five different rubber stamps. Distribute the cards to the students; then have them form groups based on the stamps on their cards.

Kristen Murphy
Laurel Elementary
New Castle, PA

Job Cards

Use the reproducible job cards on page 110 to help organize your cooperative groups. Make one set of cards per group. Cut apart the cards, glue them on tagboard, and color and laminate if desired. Fold each card on the dotted line to create a stand-up card. Discuss with students the responsibilities described on each card. At the start of each group activity, give each team a set of cards to use as handy reminders. When you're ready for students to switch jobs, simply have them swap cards!

Maxine Pincott and Peggi Savage—Gr. 4
Oliver Ellsworth School, Windsor, CT

Task
• REPORTER •

1. Reads instructions.
2. Reviews record sheets.
3. Summarizes findings and reports to the class.

REPORTER

Zipper Grouping

Try this zippy idea to sort students into groups and assign different roles. First, direct students to form a single-file line. Have the first student in line step off to the right and the second child to the left. Continue this pattern—as if the line were a zipper being unzipped—to create two lines. Repeat this process with each line to form a total of four lines. Assign the members of each line a specific group job or role, such as recorder. Then form cooperative groups by taking one student from each of the four lines. In a zip, students are sorted and assigned!

Shane Sitorius, Emerson Middle School, Bakersfield, CA

Pick a Partner, Any Partner

Looking for a new way to pair partners for class activities? Simply take a photo of each student; then cut out each child's body and mount it on a 2" x 4" strip of paper. Laminate the paper strips. When you need to pair students, hold the photo strips facedown in your hand like a deck of cards and allow each student to draw a strip. What a picture-perfect way to place students into pairs!

Christine King—Gr. 5
The Grammar School
Wilbraham, MA

Group Work

Fun and Fair Grouping

Assign students to cooperative groups in a snap with this nifty idea. First, instruct each child to divide a sheet of notebook paper into six sections as shown. Divide your class into equally sized groups. Give each student in Group 1 a red marker, each child in Group 2 a green marker, and so on until each group has been given a different-colored marker. Have students move around the room, forming groups comprised of children with different-colored markers. After groups are formed, have each student sign box 1 on his sheet and on his groupmates' sheets. Then have students form new groups in the same manner, filling out box 2. Continue until each student has filled all six boxes on his sheet, resulting in a list of six different groups in which he can work. Direct each student to keep his log in a notebook at his desk. When you assign group work, just roll a die and have students form the corresponding groups.

Barbara Ann Chastain—Gr. 4
Robinson Elementary, Aurora, MO

Group 1	Group 2
Josh	Josh
Lauren	Paul
Ryan	Jessica
Lizzie	Robbie

Group 3	Group 4
Josh	Josh
Cindy	Mark
Nancy	Vicky
Jack	Richie

Group 5	Group 6
Josh	Josh
Molly	Carol
Hannah	Robert
Michael	Samantha

Choosing Groups

As an alternative to assigning groups, I sometimes divide my class of 30 students using Popsicle sticks. I color-code the bottoms of these sticks so that there are six each of red, blue, green, brown, and yellow. I keep the Popsicle sticks in a cup with the colored portion placed down. I then walk around the room as each student draws one stick from the cup. Students who draw the same color are in the same group. For some reason, when students know that the groups are randomly selected, they don't complain as much about being separated from their friends.

Beth Gress, Crosby Elementary School, Harrison, OH

The person with the longest hair will be the...

The person wearing the most colorful shirt will be the...

The person with the longest last name will be the...

The person with the shortest pinky finger will be the...

The person with the smallest hand will be the...

The person whose clothes have the greatest number of buttons will be the...

The person who most recently ate french fries will be the...

The person sitting closest to the door will be the...

Group Starter Cards

Make introducing cooperative activities and assigning group roles a cinch with these ready-to-use starter cards! Use a blue pen to program the front of an index card with a group warm-up, such as "What do you think of today's television cartoons?" or "Describe a dream vacation you could take this month." On the back of the card, use a red pen to assign group roles according to unique attributes (see the samples at left). Make eight to ten of these cards. Then laminate the cards and store them on a large metal ring. Now starting a group activity and assigning jobs is a snap!

Callie Carman—Gr. 4, Glendale, AZ

Individualized Instruction

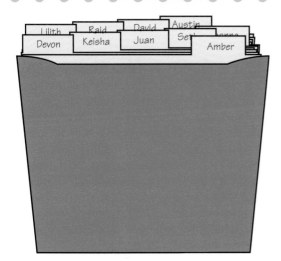

Reinforcement Folders

Meeting the individual needs of your students is just a folder away with this easy idea! Label a file folder for each student; then place the folders in a file box. Each day place a couple of reproducible activities—ones that provide reinforcement of a needed skill and can be completed independently—in each child's folder. When a student completes an activity, have him put it back in his folder for you to evaluate later.

Elaine Kaplan—Grs. 3 & 4, Laurel Plains School, New City, NY

Spelling S-u-c-c-e-s-s

What do you do with your spelling program when your students have a wide range of ability levels? Each Friday send home a list of next week's spelling words with your students; then give a pretest on the following Monday. Give students who can spell all of the words (or who miss only one word) a more challenging individualized list. During the week, some students will study the original list, while others work on the more challenging words. Two lists spell success in a classroom of wide-ranging ability levels!

Laura A. Sunley—Gr. 4, Brown Elementary, Hilliard, OH

Book Clubs to the Rescue!

"I'm planning a unit on space, but some of my students can't read the books I have on that topic!" Sound familiar? Solve this problem with the help of book clubs. Use the bonus points collected with your students' orders to purchase different levels of reading material for the units you teach. (Also check with teachers in grade levels above and below yours to see if you can order appropriate books from their book clubs.) With this idea, you'll soon have multi-leveled book collections on the topics you teach.

Cheryl Radley, Lake Norman Elementary, Mooresville, NC

Book Club

Cheryl Radley
Lake Normal Elementary
Mooresville, NC

Individualized Instruction

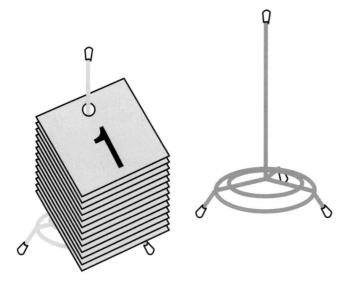

Take a Number

To keep students from standing in line at my desk when they need help, I bought two rubber-tipped spindles—a gold one and a silver one. I also punched a hole in the top of each dated page in a desk calendar. I stacked the calendar pages—with 1 on top—on the gold spindle. When a student needs individual help, she takes a number from the gold spindle. When I call that student's number, she comes to my desk and places her number on the silver spindle. Students know that they will get the help they need, plus they never have to stand in line.

Betty Edwards—Gr. 4, Tyson Elementary, Springdale, AR

Accent on Reading

Try teaching a language arts or reading skill (such as main idea or punctuation) to your entire class; then vary the independent work according to your students' reading levels. Create a file of independent activities—pulled from different levels of reading materials and resources such as *The Mailbox®* magazine—on each specific skill so that students can practice that skill using materials that are on their reading levels.

Cindy Ward—Resource, Yellow Branch Elementary, Rustburg, VA

Beg and Borrow

If several of your students are working below grade level, send out an SOS to friends who are primary grade teachers! Beg or borrow manipulatives, games, workbooks, and other appropriate items to use with your less able students. You may find your colleague is willing to swap her materials for higher-level ones for her more capable students.

Teresa Williams—Gr. 4, Silver Creek School
Hope, British Columbia, Canada

Audiocassettes to the Rescue!

- Modify homework assignments by recording content area textbook material (social studies, science, health, etc.) on audiocassette tapes. Students who aren't reading on grade level can follow along with their classmates and still learn valuable information. *Cindy Ward—Resource, Yellow Branch Elementary, Rustburg, VA*

- Individualize assessment by tape-recording tests. Students may listen to a test with a Walkman tape player and then record their answers. *Michelle Sears—Gr. 4, Cary Elementary, Cary, NC*

- Record individualized spelling and reading exercises on audiocassette tapes each week. Label and store the tapes, along with supplemental activities, in Ziploc bags. Two or three students listen to the tapes at a time, with each child challenged at his level. With headphones, no one knows how "easy" or "hard" someone else's activities are! *Cindy Dixon, Thomson Middle School, Thomson, GA*

Social Studies
Chapter 3, pages 94–111

Manageable Math

How can you manage a heterogeneous classroom and still provide for individual progress in math? Provide each student with a 9" x 12" envelope labeled "[Name]'s Math in Progress." Copy math puzzles, mind bogglers, and fun reproducibles of varying difficulty levels to place in these envelopes according to each child's ability. When you need to provide individual or small-group instruction, ask the other students to work on the materials in their envelopes.

Ann Redmond—Gr. 4, Lower Salford Elementary
Harleysville, PA

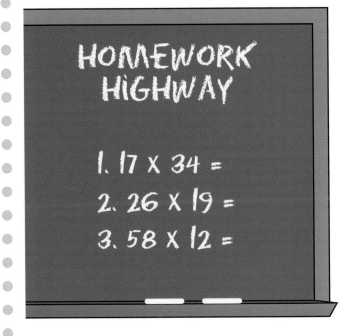

HOMEWORK HIGHWAY

1. 17 x 34 =
2. 26 x 19 =
3. 58 x 12 =

Homework Highway

Once I feel that most of my students understand a teacher-directed math lesson, we travel down the "Homework Highway." I write three related problems on the chalkboard. Students who can solve all three problems on their own are given the green light to start on their math homework. Students who miss any of the three problems on the board join me at the "Service Plaza" (my round table) for further one-on-one help. Once students master the skill, they too can begin their homework.

Kathy Fisler—Gr. 5, Wekiva Elementary, Longwood, FL

Individualized Instruction

Take-Home Study Guide

Help lower-achieving students find success with this simple study technique. After you've finished a lesson and made an assignment, briefly meet one-on-one with each underachieving child. Ask the student to restate in his own words the steps needed to complete the assignment. As the child talks, transcribe his instructions onto paper, pointing out any corrections and drawing illustrations as needed. Have the student take the paper home to use as a study guide (and to provide his parent with an easy-to-read explanation of the assignment). Use the same paper for the entire week so the student can see how each day's lesson builds on the previous one.

Cara N. Duffy—Gr. 5, Sweetser Elementary, Sweetser, IN

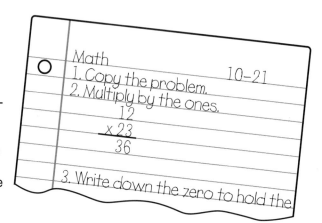

Parent Partners

Parent volunteers are the best tools for individualizing instruction! Ask parents to help monitor cooperative-learning activities, tutor individual students, read questions orally to individual children, and reinforce basic skills. Anything is possible with a better student-adult ratio!

Michelle Sears—Gr. 4, Cary Elementary, Cary, NC

Tutor Time

Wishing you could clone yourself so you could reach every student who needs one-on-one help? When there doesn't seem to be enough of you to go around, periodically schedule a "tutor time" session. During this period, pair each struggling student with a capable classmate who can "reteach" the skill to him. Everyone wins with this activity: The tutor reinforces her own skills by helping a classmate, while the previously confused child gets the help he needs.

Kirsten Sasaki, Copiague Middle School, Long Island, NY

Name _____ Reaction form

What's Your Reaction?

Title of piece: _____

Write your reaction to this piece in the space provided.

Student	Teacher	Parent

©The Education Center, Inc. • *500 Classroom Tips* • TEC60849

Name _____ Reaction form

What's Your Reaction?

Title of piece: _____

Write your reaction to this piece in the space provided.

Student	Teacher	Parent

©The Education Center, Inc. • *500 Classroom Tips* • TEC60849

Note to the teacher: Use with "Creative-Writing Portfolios" on page 86.

Name_____ Self-evaluation

Was I on Target Today?

How responsible were you today? Think about the behaviors and attitudes you exhibited. Write "yes" or "no" in each box.

	MON.	TUES.	WED.	THURS.	FRI.
FOCUS Did I concentrate and pay attention?					
PARTICIPATION Did I contribute in class and/or in my group?					
GOOD WORK HABITS Did I put forth my best effort?					
POSITIVE ATTITUDE Did I believe in myself?					
INDEPENDENT SKILLS When working alone, did I use my time wisely?					
CITIZENSHIP Did I treat others with respect?					

Name_____ Self-evaluation

Was I on Target Today?

How responsible were you today? Think about the behaviors and attitudes you exhibited. Write "yes" or "no" in each box.

	MON.	TUES.	WED.	THURS.	FRI.
FOCUS Did I concentrate and pay attention?					
PARTICIPATION Did I contribute in class and/or in my group?					
GOOD WORK HABITS Did I put forth my best effort?					
POSITIVE ATTITUDE Did I believe in myself?					
INDEPENDENT SKILLS When working alone, did I use my time wisely?					
CITIZENSHIP Did I treat others with respect?					

Note to the teacher: Use with "Student Self-Evaluations" on page 91.

My Self-Evaluation

Name _____ Date _____

Directions: After reviewing your portfolio for this grading period, complete the following statements:

1 During this grading period, I enjoyed _____ the

most because _____.

2 I think I made the most progress with _____.

3 I still need to work on _____

_____

4 My effort on my assignments has been _____

_____

5 My favorite book I read during this grading period was _____

_____

6 One goal I have for the next grading period is to _____

_____

7 I spend about _____ on homework each night.

8 I think I need to improve in the following areas*:

☐ following directions   ☐ participating in class discussions

☐ completing work on time   ☐ cooperating in groups

☐ bringing supplies to class   ☐ listening in class

☐ neatness   ☐ spending more time on homework

☐ obeying class rules   ☐ _____

* Remember: We *all* have areas in which we need to improve. Be honest.

Note to the teacher: Use with "Self-Evaluation Reports" on page 91.

TASKS
• PRINCIPAL INVESTIGATOR •

1. Supervises assembly of materials and equipment.
2. First to put materials to use.
3. Makes sure all group members have an equal chance to participate.

PRINCIPAL INVESTIGATOR

©The Education Center, Inc. • *500 Classroom Tips* • TEC60849

TASKS
• MATERIALS MANAGER •

1. Collects and returns materials.
2. Reports any damaged or missing materials to the teacher.
3. Gathers additional information from the teacher.

MATERIALS MANAGER

©The Education Center, Inc. • *500 Classroom Tips* • TEC60849

TASKS
• REPORTER •

1. Reads instructions.
2. Reviews record sheets.
3. Summarizes findings and reports to the class.

REPORTER

©The Education Center, Inc. • *500 Classroom Tips* • TEC60849

TASKS
• DATA COLLECTOR •

1. Records data and observations on the group worksheet(s).
2. Returns the worksheet(s) to the teacher.
3. Checks activity results.

DATA COLLECTOR

©The Education Center, Inc. • *500 Classroom Tips* • TEC60849

Contents

Class Puzzle

In addition to rewarding individual efforts, I like to honor my students as a class for responsible behavior. I begin by having students choose a celebration they would like to work toward, such as a pizza party. I then draw and laminate a picture that represents the party, such as a pizza. I cut the picture into ten to 12 pieces, which I store with a roll of tape in a Ziploc bag. Whenever I catch the class as a whole on task or cooperating, I choose someone to select a piece and add it to the puzzle. The day after the puzzle has been completed, we choose a new theme and celebrate!

Eileen J. Harford—Grs. 5 & 6
Orchard Middle School, Solon, OH

Hallway Handoff

This game is a surefire way to keep hallway noise levels down—and keep students smiling! Before your class leaves the room, give the last child in line a mini football. As students walk in the hallways, have them silently pass the ball to each other toward the front of the line. If you notice someone talking, have students pass the ball back two people. If the first student in line is holding the ball when you reach your destination, the class scores seven points. If the ball doesn't reach the first student, then you score the touchdown. Award points after each hallway trip and keep a running score throughout the day. The team with more points at the end of the day is the class champ!

Renee Cook—Gr. 5, Westport Elementary, Springfield, MO

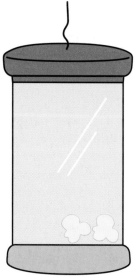

Beat the Teacher

To keep my students motivated to be on their best behavior all year long, I play a game with them called Beat the Teacher. First, I cut what looks like the top and bottom of a jar from construction paper. Then I connect the two cutouts with a five-foot piece of clear lamination and hang the resulting jar on one of our classroom walls. Each week I draw a gameboard in a small section of the chalkboard. One side is labeled "Miss Mertz" and the other side is labeled "Fourth Grade." As we proceed through our day, I award points to the class each time I see everyone following directions and working quietly. However, if I notice students who are off task or are being disruptive, I give myself a point. At the end of the day, if the students have "beat the teacher," I place a cutout of a treat in the jar. (I use the same treat until the jar is full.) Some treat shapes that I have used include popcorn, chocolate chip cookies, doughnuts, Popsicle treats, and ice-cream sundaes. When the jar is full, we celebrate our excellent behavior with a party featuring the treat in the jar.

Gwen Mertz—Gr. 4
Wyomissing Hills Elementary Center
Wyomissing Hills, PA

Stamp Contest

Use reward stamps to reinforce positive behavior with this first-class activity! Divide an 8½" x 11" sheet of paper into two-inch squares. Label each square with your name and a cute slogan, such as "Success Stamp." Make a class supply of these squares on colored paper and cut them apart. Give a stamp to a student each time you see him use positive behavior in your classroom. Then, each Friday, hold a contest during which students are free to place as many stamps with their names written on them as they wish inside a special container. Remind them that entering is risky, however, since all stamps which have been entered are destroyed after each contest. Choose two stamps from the container and award inexpensive/cost-free prizes—such as books, free homework passes, and snacks—to the lucky winners. Then post the winners' names on a bulletin board titled "First-Class Students!"

Helene Singer—Gr. 4, Holbrook Road School
Centereach, NY

Friday Challenge

Keep your students on task all week long by instituting a Friday Challenge. Pair up with another teacher in your grade level. On Monday, announce to students that your partner's class has challenged yours to an activity on Friday (a kickball game, a geography bee, etc.). Only students who stay on task throughout the week will be included in the challenge. You'll be amazed at the quality of work your students will produce with this easy incentive.

Eileen J. Harford—Grs. 5 & 6, Orchard Middle School, Solon, OH

Fishing for Compliments

Searching for an easy way to monitor behavior when students are away at specials like music and art? Make a supply of the fish patterns on page 163. Using blue paper, create a pond on a bulletin board or wall as shown. Also make a fishing pole with the line dangling in the pond. Tape or staple all fish in the pond. When the class goes to specials, have the line leader take a fish from the pond and give it to the specials teacher.

If the entire class demonstrates good behavior, the class catches the fish. A caught fish is brought back to the classroom and attached to the fishing pole. If the class did not catch the fish due to poor behavior, the fish is thrown back into the pond. Once all the fish have been caught, the class earns a prize.

Nikki Nicholson—Gr. 4, Donovan Elementary
Donovan, IL

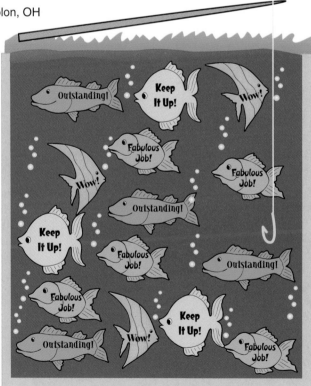

Discipline Tickets

Want to hold your students responsible for their behavior? Duplicate a discipline ticket (as shown) that can be used for both positive and negative behavior. Request that the student fill out and sign the ticket. Discuss the incident with the student, if necessary, before you sign the ticket. Store the tickets in an expanding file folder or binder. When a student accumulates a predetermined number of positive tickets, staple them together and send them home with a reward (candy, bookmark, etc.). When a student accumulates a predetermined number of negative tickets, phone parents and send the copies home. Have parents sign the tickets and return them to you. Do this on a weekly basis so students start fresh each Monday. With this idea, you will have a written record of each student's behavior, which comes in handy at conference time.

Pamela Doerr—Substitute, Elizabethtown School District
Elizabethtown, PA

Discipline Ticket

Date: _____

Name: _____

Behavior: _____

_____

_____

_____

Student Signature: _____

Teacher Signature: _____

Parent Signature: _____

Race the Clock

Draw a clock face on poster board; then laminate it. For each day that no one is placed in time-out or is sent to the office, place a sticker on one of the clock face numbers. When all 12 numbers are covered by stickers, reward the entire class with extra recess or a video party.

Beverly Langland—Gr. 5, Trinity Christian Academy, Jacksonville, FL

Name _____

You're Great!

Catch 'em Doing Good!

At the beginning of the school year, I give each of my students an incentive chart with 20 spaces. Each time a student exhibits responsible behavior, I stamp one or two spaces on his chart. When the student has earned 20 stamps, he can cash in his chart for a special privilege, such as an extra half hour of computer time. Or he can choose to fill another sheet and cash in all 40 spaces for a reward of even greater value, such as a night of no homework, a chance to serve as another teacher's helper, or joining another class for recess. Focusing on positive behaviors—now that's motivating!

Mary Pio—Gr. 4, Madie Ives Elementary, Miami, FL

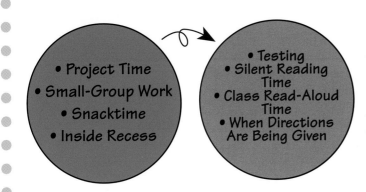

- Project Time
- Small-Group Work
- Snacktime
- Inside Recess

- Testing
- Silent Reading Time
- Class Read-Aloud Time
- When Directions Are Being Given

Red Light, Green Light

How do you quickly remind students when and when not to talk in class? Simply use the red light-green light system! Have students brainstorm a list of times when it's okay to talk softly in class. List these times on a large green posterboard circle. Then brainstorm a list of times when it's not okay to talk in class. List these times on a large red posterboard circle. Glue the circles together back-to-back; then display the stoplight in the room. Throughout the day flip to the appropriate color as a reminder.

Rosemary Linden—Gr. 4, Royal Valley Elementary, Hoyt, KS

Invitation to Good Behavior

Improve student behavior every week with this invitation to success! On Monday give each student a blank index card. Have him design an invitation on the card to a special Friday reward such as extra recess or a homework-free night. Collect the invitations and place them on a bulletin board labeled "Invitation to Good Behavior!" Next, outline the behavior that is expected in order for a student to earn the reward. When a child's behavior doesn't match your expectations, have her punch a hole in her invitation. Remove a student's card from the board after two punches and remind her that she gets a fresh start on Monday. Then, on Friday, reward those students who still have their cards on the board with the special treat.

Kim Vader, Anchor Bay Middle School
Mt. Clemens, MI

Turn the Tables

All too often the students creating behavior problems are the ones getting all the recognition. Turn the tables around by making your well-behaved students the stars of your classroom. While teaching, identify those students who are on task by putting their names on the board. Put a star by each name. Add stars to the names as the students continue to behave. Whenever you need classroom helpers, refer to the list of starred students. Recognizing the students who are following directions will encourage those not on task to turn their behavior around. Plan special classroom activities to celebrate days when the entire class is starred.

Mary F. Harding—Gr. 4
Thomas J. Pappas School for Homeless Children
Phoenix, AZ

The Jewel System

For a fun and effective positive discipline program, try the Jewel System. Give each student a 35 mm film container labeled with his name. At the beginning of the week, fill each student's container with eight jewels (inexpensive plastic beads). The first behavior warning is free. If a student gets a second warning, he loses a jewel. The amount of jewels remaining each Friday determines the amount of free time earned. Students who have kept all eight jewels receive a special treat. Refill each container on Monday with eight jewels so every student has a fresh start.

Shelly Lennon—Gr. 4, Santa Catalina School, Monterey, CA

Chance Cards

Do your students like surprises? If so, try using the element of surprise in your positive discipline program. Give each student an index card with her name on it. At the beginning of each class, have students put the cards on the corners of their desks. To reinforce a student who behaves well, is prepared for class, follows the rules, or lends a helping hand, place a motivating stamp or sticker on her card. When a student has earned 15 stamps, let her draw a Chance Card. Chance Cards are laminated and decorated index cards that are labeled with prizes or privileges. Half the fun for the students is not knowing what prizes they will draw.

Darby A. Herlong—Gr. 5, Wateree Elementary, Lugoff, SC

Hurrah for 100!

Hurrah for 100!

Encourage excellent class cooperation and improved behavior around the school with this "complimentary" idea. On a piece of poster board, create a chart with 100 boxes and title it as shown. Then laminate the chart. Each time your students receive a compliment from a staff member for good behavior in the hallway or another area of the building, use a wipe-off marker to draw a star in the next available box on the chart. When the class earns 100 stars, celebrate with a "Hurrah for 100!" party. Or let students have lunch in the classroom, extra recess, or a homework-free night. After the celebration, wipe off the chart and start again, challenging students to earn compliments for improved behavior in another area.

Amy Taylor—Gr. 4, Charlesmont Elementary
Dundalk, MD

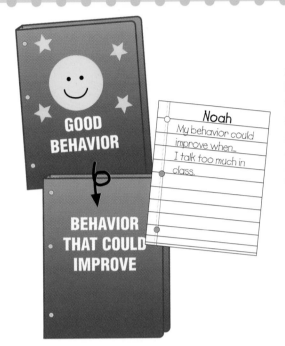

The Flip Side

To encourage students to be responsible for their behavior, decorate the front of a three-ring binder with the title "Good Behavior." Flip the binder; then label the blank cover "Behavior That Could Improve." Have each student write her name and "I showed good behavior when…" at the top of a sheet of paper. Bind these pages alphabetically in the front of the binder. Next, have each student write her name and "My behavior could improve when…" at the top of a second sheet of paper. Flip the binder and bind these pages inside. When a child demonstrates good behavior, invite her to write about it on her page in the front of the binder. If she displays poor behavior, have the student write about how she could improve on her page in the back of the binder.

Pat Twohey—Gr. 4
Old County Road School
Smithfield, RI

Simon Says, "Silence, Please!"

To control the noise level of my students both inside and outside our classroom, I use a "Follow my lead if you're listening" strategy. First, I quietly say, "Raise your hand if you're listening." Then I give a command such as "Put your hands on your head if you're listening." I continue with simple directions (similar to the children's game Simon Says) until the entire class is listening and playing along. The follow-the-leader fun always captures my students' attention!

Caroline Johnson—Gr. 5, Citrus Elementary, Upland, CA

Die-Cut Coupons

Many schools have die-cut machines for cutting out patterns and shapes. These cute cutouts can be useful in your behavior-management program. Select four or five patterns that have room for writing, and make several cutouts of each pattern. Program each cutout with a different reward and place them in a bowl. When a student demonstrates great behavior, let her pick a cutout from the bowl.

Katie Kasar
Carollton Elementary
Oak Creek, WI

"Fry" Your Best

Here's a way to get your students cookin' on good behavior. Ask a fast-food restaurant to donate french fry boxes, one for each child in your room. Write each child's name on a separate box. Make four french fries for each child by spraying yellow paint on pinch clothespins. After the clothespins have dried, clip them on the boxes. Staple the boxes to a bulletin board with your classroom rules and consequences such as these:

- one fry removed—warning
- two fries removed—ten minutes of time-out
- three fries removed—15 minutes of time-out
- four fries removed—phone conference with parent

At the end of each day, replace all fries that had to be removed and give each child a fresh start the next day.

Sue Townsend—Gr. 4, Brandon Elementary, Brandon, MS

Reach for the Stars

Are you tired of giving little trinkets for rewards? Make or purchase an incentive chart with 20 boxes for each student. Post the charts on a bulletin board or wall. Cut large stars out of yellow construction paper and laminate them for durability. Write a different privilege on each star; then tack all of the stars to another bulletin board. Whenever a student demonstrates good behavior or follows directions, place a sticker on his chart. After a student has received 20 stickers, let him choose a star from the Reward Board.

Cindy Wood—Grs. 5–6, St. Clare Elementary, Waveland, MS

The Great Behavior Raffle

To motivate good behavior and homework completion, I started the Great Behavior Raffle. On Friday each student who completed all work and exhibited responsible behavior gets to place his name in my raffle box. Once a month I pull a name out of the box and reward the lucky student with an inexpensive gift. I also photograph the child holding his prize; then I mount the photo on a piece of poster board that is displayed in my classroom year-round. This display is a great visual reminder of how doing the right thing pays off!

Christel S. Pedota—Gr. 5
St. Agnes of Bohemia School
Chicago, IL

Post-it Brand Note Coupons

Looking for a system of positive rewards that requires a minimum of time and effort? At the beginning of the day, give a Post-it Brand note to each student. Have the student put his name on the note and keep it on top of his desk for the day. When a student displays appropriate behavior, stamp the paper with a positive message. When the student earns three stamps, the paper becomes a coupon redeemable for a treat or a small reward at the end of the day. Allow students to earn more than one coupon a day. To extend the activity, have students put their coupons in a jar for a grand prize drawing at the end of the week, month, or grading period.

Linda C. Buerklin—Substitute Teacher
Monroe Township Schools
Williamstown, NJ

Counting the Days

Similar to the accident-free signs that are often posted outside factories, I have a discipline report sign that lists how many days it's been since I've had to send a discipline letter to a parent or to the principal. This motivates the students as they watch the number grow and grow!

Julie Granchelli, Lockport, NY

Pickle Jar Lottery

Pickle Jar Lottery is an incentive activity that promotes good behavior in my classroom. The object of the activity is for students to get caught being good. Once or twice a week, I have Pickle Day. The children don't know which day I will choose. At the end of the day, I hand out paper pickles to students who did not get their names on the board and who completed all assignments on time. Students write their names on the pickles and put them in a pickle jar. At the end of the month, I draw a pickle from the jar. The child whose name is on the pickle gets to choose a prize from the treasure chest. My students love the excitement of our monthly drawings. And I love the good behavior in my classroom!

Tina R. Sutton—Gr. 4, Robinson Elementary, Dawsonville, GA

Behavior

Behavior Basket

Are you becoming a basket case looking for a timely way to motivate and reward your students' good behavior and work habits? Look no further! Copy a seasonal cutout for each of your students and distribute them. For example, use pumpkins, leaves, or apples in the fall; snowmen, trees, or bells in the winter; and eggs, flowers, or shamrocks in the spring. Have each student decorate and write her name on the cutout. As good behavior or work habits are observed, add the student's cutout to a large basket (real or a bulletin board cutout). When all names are in the basket, reward the class with a special treat.

Sharon Sealts—Substitute Teacher
Columbus Grove, OH

"CBG"—Caught Being Good

I enjoy catching my students being good. When I see a student making a good decision, helping a friend, or following directions, I give him a CBG (Caught Being Good) award. The award is a colorful plastic clothespin that I attach to outstanding papers, shirtsleeves, or desks. Sometimes I even hide one in a coat pocket with a note attached for a neat surprise! Students redeem their CBGs at the CBG Store for free homework passes, pencils, extra test points, free time, or other rewards. Not only do I enjoy catching my students being good, but they also enjoy being caught too!

Sheila K. Bowman—Gr. 4, Victory Christian School, Albuquerque, NM

Three Strikes and You're Out!

Looking for a way to control the noise level of your class when doing fun activities or playing games? Draw a strike box on the chalkboard as shown. Explain that if students get too loud, the class will get a strike. After three strikes, it's time to end the activity. My students like this method and often ask to use the strike box when the noise level begins to rise.

Laura Reeb—Gr. 4
Anderson Mill Elementary
Austin, TX

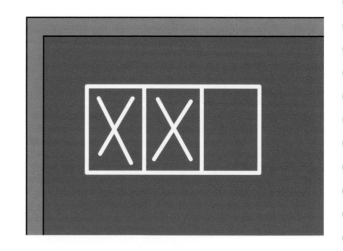

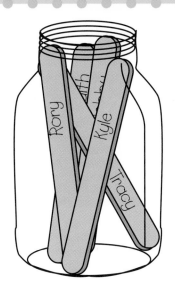

Popsicle Stick Incentive

In the morning, I give each student in my class a Popsicle stick labeled with her name. If a child breaks a class behavior rule anytime during the day, she turns in her stick to me. About ten minutes before dismissal, a helper collects the sticks from students who were able to keep them all day. I put the sticks in a jar, shake them up, and draw one. The winner receives a pencil, eraser, candy treat, or other small prize. This incentive really encourages students to be responsible for their behavior. It also motivates those who lose their sticks one day to do better the next, since everyone starts fresh each day.

Pamela J. Fox—Gr. 4, Brassfield Elementary, Bixby, OK

Cooldown Cards

Have you ever put a student in time-out and then forgotten to discuss with that child why he was there? Try using Cooldown Cards (see the reproducible on page 164). These cards will help you keep track of behavior and will also give the students more responsibility for their actions. The cards have three questions for the student to answer: What's the problem? What can I do to correct the problem? Why shouldn't I be exhibiting this behavior? The student writes the answers to the questions during the time-out and discusses them with the teacher. The card is then sent home to be signed and returned by the parent. These cards are great for keeping track of a student's progress and parent communications, and for encouraging reflective thinking.

Cindy Wood—Grs. 5–6, St. Clare Elementary, Waveland, MS

"Marble-ous" Behavior

Looking for a unique way to reinforce positive behavior in your class? I purchased a maze that can be set up in different ways to control the movement of a marble as it makes its way to the track's end. I place a collection container at the maze end. Then, as a class, we decide upon a desired behavior. Each time I observe a student exhibiting that behavior, I allow that student to place a marble in the maze. When the marble-collection container is full, I reward my class with a prize; then I let the student who placed the last marble in the container design a new maze so we can begin the challenge again.

Nancy Lemay
Marlboro, MA

Timer Tip

I use a great little device to get my students' attention: a small magnetic timer attached to my chalkboard. When students get a little too noisy, I simply turn on the timer. The time it takes students to settle down is the amount of time they have to wait before going out to recess or playing a game. It's amazing that students can hear that timer begin—no matter how noisy it is in the classroom! Substitute teachers find this timer especially helpful.

Debbie Patrick—Gr. 5, Park Forest Elementary, State College, PA

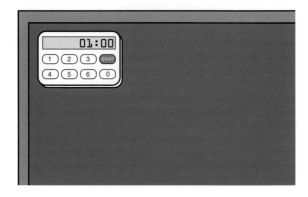

Oh, Boy—It's T.G.I.F.!

To reward students for responsible behavior, the fifth-grade teachers at our school instituted T.G.I.F., or Time for Group Interaction on Friday. Students who turn in all assignments on time during the week and do not break any class rules are invited to a 30-minute get-together on Friday afternoon. The students—who are in five different self-contained homerooms—are thrilled with the chance to socialize with buddies from other classes. Students who don't earn the chance to participate in T.G.I.F. are grouped in several of the homerooms to work on missing/incomplete assignments or to read quietly. During this time, these children have a chance to catch up with their schoolwork so they can start fresh the next week. To help reinforce the concept of making responsible decisions, we stress to students that missing T.G.I.F. isn't a punishment, but a consequence of their choices.

Therese Durhman—Gr. 5, Mountain View School, Hickory, NC

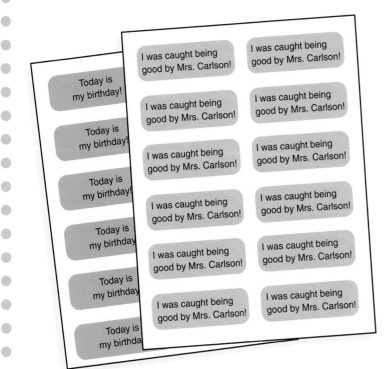

Big Kid Congrats

Congratulate students for a job well done with this timesaving incentive. Each month use your computer to make several sheets of labels as shown. When a student exhibits exemplary behavior or work habits, simply peel off a label and place it on his shirt. Not only will you avoid having to write out a note, but you'll also guarantee that the label will get home for parents to see. Plus the labels are small enough so that your "big kids" won't be embarrassed to wear them. Make additional labels that read "Today is my birthday!" to award on everyone's special day.

Lisa Carlson—Gr. 5
Dunbar Hill Elementary
Hamden, CT

Smart Choices Bucket

Smart Choices Bucket

Looking for a way to encourage students to make smart choices? Try this easy-to-implement system. Gather two equal-size, clear containers and label one "Smart Choices Bucket." Fill the other container with small incentives—such as candy, erasers, stickers, and bookmarks—that have been donated by parents. Each time the class makes a smart choice, such as standing quietly in line or following directions, acknowledge the students' actions by having each child select one incentive and place it in the Smart Choices Bucket. After all incentives have been transferred from one container to the other, equally divide the items into goodie bags for your students. Now that's a smart choice!

Laurel Nascimento and Rebecca Worst—Gr. 4
Saint Joseph School, Marietta, GA

You Can Bank on It

My students start their day with their names and two stars on a bulletin board titled "Star Students." Their goal is to keep their two stars by displaying good behavior for the day. At the end of the day, students who still have both stars earn a quarter of play money that can be spent at our classroom store. Items for sale there include bookmarks, erasers, notebooks, homework passes, and stickers. Later in the year, the students begin opening savings and checking accounts with our class bank. Eventually, I become less involved, and the students are given the responsibility of running the bank and store. This is a great way to reward good behavior and improve math skills.

Frances Jones—Gr. 4, Erwin Elementary, Hoover, AL

Stop Signs

Encourage students to put a stop to inappropriate behavior with the following idea. Cut several small stop sign shapes from red poster board. Label the signs with white chalk or crayon before laminating them. If a student misbehaves during a lesson, place a stop sign on her desk. When the behavior stops, remove the sign. If the sign is still on the desk at recess time, the student loses part or all of her recess. The stop sign serves as a silent warning without any interruption in a lesson.

Brenda Fendley—Gr. 4
Blossom Elementary
Blossom, TX

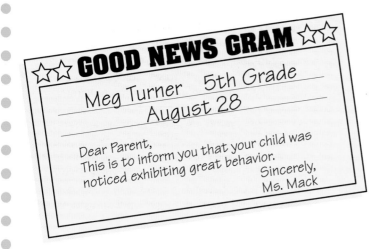

Good News Grams

Our school strives to recognize students in a positive manner, so we have instituted the Good News Gram. When a student shows respect, kindness, and consideration for others or exhibits individual progress and growth, a teacher fills out a Good News Gram and forwards it to the principal. The Good News Gram is printed on duplicate paper so that the principal can keep a copy and mail the original home to the parents. Four names each grading period are drawn from the Good News Grams collected. These four students—as well as the teachers who recognized them—are treated to a special lunch. This is a great way to promote good feelings between the students, parents, teachers, and administrators.

Nancy Curl, Olson Middle School, Tabernacle, NJ

Class Store

At the beginning of the year, I send a letter requesting parents to contribute items to the class store. For variety, I ask that 15 of one type of item be donated to the store by each parent. Inexpensive items—such as yo-yos, writing tablets, pencils, erasers, and Frisbee toys—are popular items. Each day I pass out tickets to students for positive behavior, kindness to each other, and excellent work. At the end of the week, my storekeepers (determined by the class job chart) open the class store, and students can trade in their tickets for rewards. Our store has been a big success!

Yvonne Poppen—Gr. 5, West Hills Elementary, Knoxville, TN

Thumbs-Up!

Promote positive behavior and teamwork with an incentive that's sure to earn a big thumbs-up! Decorate a sheet of poster board with a large hand and the title "Thumbs-Up!" as shown. Laminate the poster and display it in the classroom. Also purchase an inexpensive ink pad. Explain to students that each time the class receives a compliment from another teacher or shows respect to others, you will add a thumbprint to the poster. When the class earns a predetermined number of prints, reward students with a special privilege, such as a class party or field trip. Then wipe the board clean and start the challenge over again.

Louella Nygaard—Gr. 5
Isabell Bills Elementary
Colstrip, MT

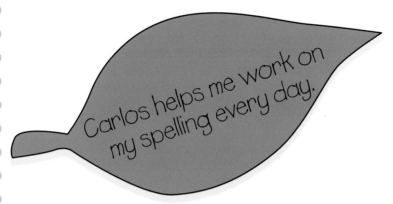

Carlos helps me work on my spelling every day.

A Giving Tree

Plant the seeds of kindness and watch students grow into givers with this "tree-men-dous" activity! First, share with students Shel Silverstein's book *The Giving Tree.* Discuss the book with students. Then display a large cutout of a bare tree on a wall. Place a container of green leaf cutouts nearby. Whenever a student is pleased by a classmate's kind word or deed, have him thank that child by writing a note on a leaf and adding it to the tree. In no time, students will see how their acts of kindness have made the tree grow greener!

Michelle Zakula—Gr. 5, Saint Roman School
Milwaukee, WI

Community Circle

Build an atmosphere of caring in your classroom by beginning each day with a special sharing time. Seat students in a circle to discuss the day's events, assignments, and goals. Then hand one child a large index card labeled with a sentence starter about a current unit. For example, if you are studying the Middle Ages, label the card "If I had lived during medieval times, I would like to have been a _____ because _____." Have the student read the sentence aloud and complete it. Then have him pass the card to the next classmate until the card has traveled around the circle. If a child doesn't wish to participate that day, allow him to say "Pass." In addition to learning more about one another, students will practice their speaking and listening skills, too!

Cynthia Pfaff—Gr. 4, Prairie View Elementary, Eden Prairie, MN

Stop, Drop, and Help

Before using cooperative learning and peer teaching in the classroom, teach students *how* to help each other. Introduce the Stop-Drop-and-Help method: Turn your paper over (stop), put your pencil down (drop), and turn to face the person who needs assistance (help). Teach students to coach one another by rephrasing questions, giving hints or clues, and using encouraging words. Display the method on a classroom poster, along with a sign on each student's desk, as reminders. Students will enjoy helping each other, and your job will become a little easier too!

Kimberly Marinelli—Gr. 5
La Barriere Crossings School
Winnipeg, Manitoba, Canada

Stop-Drop-Help!
1. Rephrase questions.
2. Give hints or clues.
3. Use encouraging words.

Class Community

The Places You'll Go!

Give students a chance to build each other's self-esteem with an unbeatable bookmaking project! First, read aloud Dr. Seuss's *Oh, the Places You'll Go!* After sharing the book, have each student staple several sheets of unlined paper inside a folded 12" x 18" sheet of construction paper. Direct the student to title her book *"Oh, the Places [student's name] Will Go!"* Then have her use crayons or markers to decorate the cover with drawings related to what she'd like to be when she grows up.

Next, ask each student to share some of her life's dreams with the class. After each child has shared, have students circulate around the room signing each classmate's book with a positive sentence about her potential success in the future. Make sure that you add a compliment to each book as well!

Cecilia C. Harkey—Grs. K–5 Academically Gifted
Rock Springs School, Denver, NC

Here's George!

To help your class consider the impact of an unkind word, tell students a story about "George." Show the class a large picture of George—one that you've drawn and colored on a piece of art paper. Describe a typical day in George's life and how some children say unkind things about him. Ask students to provide examples of unkind remarks. As they do, slowly crumple up George's picture until it's wadded into a small ball. Then tell how George meets some very nice children who make kind remarks about him. As students share examples, straighten George's picture until it's as flat as possible. Instruct classes to observe the picture. Explain that although George now feels better about himself, the evidence of the unkind words remains. Ask, "Has this ever happened to you? How did you feel? How do you think George feels? How can we keep this from happening to someone?" Display George's picture throughout the year to encourage students to season their words to one another with kindness.

Charylene Goin—Gr. 5, Mission Glen Elementary, Sugarland, TX

Kindness Bowl

Reward student kindness by placing a decorated goldfish bowl on your desk. When you catch a student performing an act of kindness, tell the student to put his name on a slip of paper and place it in the Kindness Bowl. At the end of the grading period, have a drawing. The person whose name is drawn receives a special reward.

Susan Kesler—Gr. 4
Montfort Academy
Fredericksburg, VA

Class Mail System

If you never thought you'd allow note passing in class, think again! Have each student staple together the sides of a file folder and personalize the folder. Then staple the folders to a bulletin board to use as mailboxes. After establishing rules such as those listed, allow students to write and mail friendly letters to each other during free time. (If a student misuses her mail privilege, remove her mailbox from the board for a predetermined length of time.) Periodically slip a small treat into each mailbox as a reward for good behavior or for meeting an individual or class goal.

Debra Baucom—Gr. 5
New Hope Elementary
Columbus, MS

Mail System Rules

1. Write only positive messages.
2. Use friendly letter format.
3. Write letters and check your mailbox <u>only</u> after you've completed your work.
4. Do not look in a classmate's mailbox.

Positive Posters

Each Monday, I display a large poster with the caption "Student of the Week" followed by a student's name. During the week, that student's classmates write positive comments about him or her on slips of paper; then they tape the slips to the poster. I add my own comments too. On Friday, the student of the week draws a new name to feature on next week's poster. Students keep their posters as keepsakes.

Virginia McWilliams—Gr. 5, R. E. Thompson School, Tuscumbia, AL

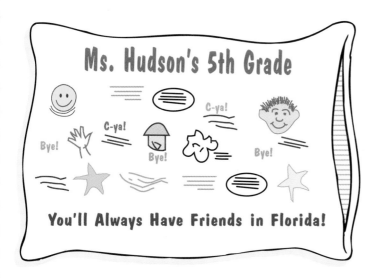

Sweet Dreams Pillow

Do you have a student who is moving or facing a long period of recuperation? Then this gift idea is perfect for letting that child know her classroom family will miss her! Purchase a white pillowcase and fabric crayons. Use the crayons to write a brief message across the top of the pillowcase as shown. Then allow students to decorate the remaining space with their signatures, pictures, and brief notes. Set the design on the pillowcase by following the crayon manufacturer's directions. Then present the gift at a farewell party. Every time the student lays her head on the decorated pillowcase, she'll recall all the terrific friends in her classroom family.

Jaimie K. Hudson, Pace, FL

Jen helped Tina clean her desk.

The Happy Spy

Happy Spies

My "Happy Spies" are always on the lookout for good deeds! I keep a decorated container with a removable, slitted lid on my desk. When a good deed happens, an observer (or recipient of the deed) records it on a slip of paper and signs the slip "The Happy Spy." Students place the slips of paper in the container. At the end of the week, I share the contents of the container with the class. Students love to hear these anonymous observations!

Chris Christensen—Gr. 4
Doris Hancock Elementary
Las Vegas, NV

You Light Up My Life!

Take time to recognize students for the kind acts they do and the special kids they are with this bright idea. Periodically schedule a Light Up My Life session. Arrange students in a circle and play soft background music. Begin the ceremony by completing the following sentence: "_____ lights up my life because _____." Then pass an unlit candle to that student and have him continue the process. Before ending the ceremony, make sure that each student in the circle is recognized.

Michelle Zakula, Saint Roman School, Milwaukee, WI

Insult-Free Zone

Ask the students if they've ever seen Drug-Free Zone or Smoke-Free Zone signs. Have students explain what these signs mean and their purposes. Then ask the class what it feels like to be insulted or put down. Share with students how insults and put-downs can hurt the entire class; then guide the students in declaring your classroom an Insult-Free Zone. Have students create signs to post around the room as reminders. Throughout the year, if a student or teacher catches someone insulting another person, he says, "Ouch!" The person who expressed the insult then owes the classmate who received it a compliment.

Mary F. Harding—Gr. 4
Thomas J. Pappas School for Homeless Children
Phoenix, AZ

STOP
This Class Is an Insult-Free Zone.

What's in a Name?

Build class spirit and identity early in the year with this group activity. First, have small teams of students brainstorm and list possible names for your class. Suggest that each team establish criteria for narrowing its list to just one name. Next, allow each team to nominate one name from its list and share its merits with the class. Then have the class vote to select the class name. Have one team design a banner incorporating the winning name. Or hold a contest to design a T-shirt sporting the name. Also order name-related stickers or labels to use on all class newsletters and other handouts. What's in a name? Plenty of class pride, that's what!

Lori Brandman—Gr. 5
Shallowford Falls Elementary
Marietta, GA

Role-Playing to the Rescue!

Troubleshoot small problems before they escalate into larger ones with this role-playing activity. At periodic class meetings, have students brainstorm issues that bother them, such as having no one to play with at recess or not getting along with someone. List the issues on the board and divide students into groups. Then assign each group a different issue to resolve. Have the group discuss the issue and role-play one possible solution for the class.

Michelle Zakula—Gr. 5, Saint Roman School, Milwaukee, WI

We Are Family!

This spirited bulletin board will leave no doubt that a classroom is a lot like a family! First, invite students to bring in photographs of themselves from babyhood on up. Display the photos on a brightly covered board titled "We Are Family!" Add photos of yourself to the board as well. Use this family album display to start a discussion about how a classroom and a family are alike and different. Replace all the pictures about every six weeks to maintain interest.

Latasha Johnson—Gr. 4
Kittrell School
Readyville, TN

The Pencil Box

Help students see that they need each other's individual strengths with this eye-opening activity. Provide each group of four with the following materials: a pencil box (or other container) containing a ruler, scissors, an eraser, and a golf pencil; a sheet of paper for each group member. Then have students follow these steps:

1. Choose one object from the pencil box. This is your "strength."
2. Take one sheet of paper.
3. Using *only* your strength, divide the paper into six equal parts. You are *not* allowed to share your strength with others in your group.

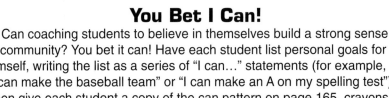

Next, ask students, "How were you able to individually complete the task? Was it easy or hard? What would help you complete the task more accurately?"

Assign the same task again, giving only one sheet of paper to each group. Allow each student to share his strength with the rest of his group to complete the task. Students will quickly see that they need each other's strengths to get the job done accurately and effectively.

Tammy S. Edwards—Gr. 5
Stanwood Elementary
Scottdale, PA

"Soup-er" Read-Alouds

Supplement your daily read-aloud time by sharing excerpts from books in the Chicken Soup series. Use these stories about love, kindness, compassion, and giving to reinforce important life skills you want to build in your classroom community.

Aden Wooten—Grs. 3–5, Intermediate Multiage, Alcoa Elementary, Alcoa, TN

Dustin Smith

I
CAN
turn in my
homework
everyday   .

You Bet I Can!

Can coaching students to believe in themselves build a strong sense of community? You bet it can! Have each student list personal goals for himself, writing the list as a series of "I can…" statements (for example, "I can make the baseball team" or "I can make an A on my spelling test"). Then give each student a copy of the can pattern on page 165, crayons, scissors, and tape. Have the student write one of his goals on the pattern. Next, have him decorate the can, cut it out, and tape it to his desktop. Suggest that he repeat the statement on the pattern to himself several times each day. When he accomplishes that goal, have the student cross it off his list. Then hand him another can pattern to label with a second goal on his list.

Aden Wooten—Grs. 3–5, Intermediate Multiage, Alcoa Elementary, Alcoa, TN

The Sky's the Limit!

Here's a lofty idea that sends self-esteem soaring! As a class, brainstorm positive statements that could make a student feel good about herself or her ability to do something well. List students' responses on the board. Next, make a class supply of the cloud pattern on page 166 on different shades of blue construction paper. Give each student scissors, a copy of the cloud pattern, and a black marker. Direct the student to cut out her pattern, choose a statement from the board, and use the marker to write that statement on her cutout. Tape the clouds to your classroom ceiling so that a reassuring thought will be just an upward gaze away!

Kim Vader, Anchor Bay Middle School
Mt. Clemens, MI

I'm great at soccer.

I am a good reader.

Student Ambassadors

Welcome new students into your classroom family with this nifty idea. At the start of the school year, select two students (a boy and a girl) to serve as student ambassadors. Explain to the two ambassadors that their duties will include such tasks as showing new students around the school, sitting with them at lunch, introducing them to teachers and staff, etc. If desired, have the ambassadors present each new student with a goodie bag filled with items such as a T-shirt decorated with the school colors, coupons for free admission to special school events, and informational flyers about your school.

Nancy Curl, Olson Middle School, Tabernacle, NJ

Marvelous Monday

Starting off the week on a positive note is a great motivator. On Monday have each student draw the name of a classmate from a basket. Have the student write a positive note about his classmate and then deliver it. After reading the note, have the classmate store it in his special "Marvelous Monday" folder. Encourage students to pull out their folders anytime they're discouraged or need a lift. When you see a folder out on a child's desk and it's not Marvelous Monday, you'll know that somebody needs a little extra encouragement.

Dawn Helton—Gr. 4
Read-Turrentine Elementary
Silsbee, TX

Group Motivation

The Water Race

Encourage better behavior with this virtually cost-free idea that's slightly soggy but full of fun! Gather a same-size plastic container for each cooperative group. When every member of a group completes his homework or stays on task, pour one cup of water into his group's container. (To distinguish one container from another, dye the water in each container with different-colored food coloring.) Also award a cup of water for good behavior, teamwork, or any other goal you want to reinforce. Reward the first group to fill its container with a special treat. Then empty the containers and play again.

Christine Ward—Gr. 5
East Brook Middle School
Paramus, NJ

Cooperative Discipline

To maintain a positive learning environment in your classroom, try using this cooperative discipline strategy. Arrange students' desks into groups of four or five. Give points to groups for positive, cooperative behavior observed throughout the day; then record the points on a chart posted in the room. At the end of the week, reward the group with the most points. To be effective and fair, change the groups every two weeks. Once a month total all the groups' points. When 500 is reached, treat the whole class to free time, a popcorn party, or some other special activity.

Storie Brown—Gr. 4, George Weatherbee School, Hampden, ME

Co-op Cards

Motivating students to stay on task in cooperative groups can be difficult. To help increase on-task behavior, I've used Co-op Cards in my classroom for years. (See the pattern on page 167.) At the beginning of the year, give each student a card and inform him that during group work or cooperative assignments, he will get a space signed for working cooperatively, remaining on task, completing the assignment, etc. The object is to get all 12 spaces signed by the teacher. After a student completes a card, he chooses a reward and is given a new card. Rewards are determined by the class each year and listed on a chart posted in the room. When 12 students have completed cards, the entire class is rewarded with a popcorn party. The cards motivate individual students to stay on task, which benefits the whole group.

Donna Lee Wynn—Gr. 5, M. G. Clark School
Sioux City, IA

Team Points

Encourage student groups to be more responsible for their behavior with this motivating idea! Label a sheet of poster board "Team Points." For each team, attach a column of seven Velcro squares to the poster as shown. Label the rows of squares from 1 point to 6 points, leaving the bottom row unlabeled. Next, make a paper circle for each team. Label each circle with a team's name and back it with a piece of Velcro. Attach all of the circles to the bottom row of Velcro. Throughout the day, move the circles up or down the chart depending on each team's behavior. At the end of the day, count the number of points each team has earned. Give the first team to reach 40 points a reward of its choice.

Tamara Bolden—Gr. 5, County Line Elementary, Winder, GA

Your Attention, Please

Whenever my students work in small cooperative groups, I use two effective methods to get their attention for whole-class discussions. I simply call out "spaghetti" and the students must all respond with "meatballs." I usually only have to say "spaghetti" once or twice to get everyone's attention. A second method that I use is to clap a specific pattern which the students must repeat. After one or two patterns, everyone is usually quiet and attentive.

Terri Jackson—Gr. 4, Franklin Elementary, Reistertown, MD

Hugs, Hugs, and More Hugs!

To encourage good behavior in my class, I arrange my students in six groups of four desks each. Large paper numerals (1–6) hang from the ceiling above the groups so that no matter how often I regroup them, students can easily identify their group numbers. Each group also has a large coffee can covered with bright paper and labeled with the group's numeral. The cans are for storing hugs! My hugs are small strips of colorful paper labeled with the word *hugs*. Students earn hugs when any adult compliments their behavior, when they are on task, and when they exhibit good behavior throughout the school. On Monday, the hugs are counted; then students in the group with the most hugs are my helpers for the week. Even though my hugs are paper, students know that this is my way of letting them know how proud I am of their good behavior.

Sandy Carter—Gr. 5
Carpenter Elementary
Deer Park, TX

Group Motivation

Green Means "Go!"

Looking for a strategy to quickly let cooperative groups know if they're on task or not? Try laminating three circles—a red, a yellow, and a green one. During group time, drop the circles on groups' tables to indicate how they're doing. The green circle means "Go!" (you're all on task). The yellow circle means "Caution!" (take a one-minute time-out, reorganize, and change your behavior). The red circle means "Stop!" (stop and take a close look at your behavior; then try again). This warning system helps groups correct their behavior early and get back on the right track.

Karen A. Chuba—Gr. 4, Cook Hill Elementary, Wallingford, CT

Shooting for the Stars

During cooperative-group activities, my class likes shooting for the stars! To begin the lesson, I set three behavior expectations for the students. The expectations vary depending on the activity, but often include group involvement, cooperation, transition, and organization. After completing the activity, each group evaluates itself on how well group members met the expectations, with a rating scale of one through six. (Six is the highest rating a group can give itself.) Stars are given to the groups with a rating of six. Stars are golden because a six rating means a no-homework pass for each group member!

Karen A. Chuba—Gr. 4, Cook Hill Elementary, Wallingford, CT

Teamwork Tally

Promote good behavior and cooperation in group settings with the following idea. Divide students into teams; then have each group decide on a team name. Give each group a large piece of poster board to decorate with its team name, team members' names, and any decorative pictures or symbols. Award points to teams that are on task or are ready first after a transition. Also award points for positive behaviors, such as working quietly, listening, completing work on time, following directions quickly, etc. Keep track of earned points. At the end of the week, reward the winning team with a special treat or privilege. You'll be amazed at how peer pressure and cooperation keep students on task and prepared for their lessons!

Sandi Norton—Gr. 4
Valley Springs Elementary
Harrison, AR

Update Cards

Monitoring on-task behavior in cooperative learning groups without interrupting them can be tricky. Update cards can help. Make two sets of laminated cards. Label one set "This group is working nicely!" and label the other set "Too noisy!" If you see a group that is on task and working well, quietly drop the appropriate card in the middle of its table. You'll see lots of smiles from the group members, and they'll continue to work even harder. If you see a group that is too loud and not on task, do not say anything; simply drop the "Too noisy!" card in the middle of its table. The group that receives the "Too noisy!" card will immediately quiet down and get back to work. At the end of the activity, collect the cards to use again.

Dawn Tameo-Greening
Peter Thacher Middle School
Attleboro, MA

We All Scream for Ice Cream!

Divide each class into teams of five to six students each. On a bulletin board, post a large ice-cream cone for each team. Award points to teams each time a member exhibits responsible behavior, completes an assignment, shows kindness to a classmate, etc. At the end of the day, reward the team that has accumulated the most points with a paper scoop to place on its cone. When a team earns six scoops, reward it with an ice-cream treat.

Beverly Langland—Gr. 5, Trinity Christian Academy, Jacksonville, FL

The "Hole" Game

This management technique is sure to be a winner in any classroom! First, divide your students into small groups; then list the names of each group's members on a small index card. Punch a hole in each card, thread string through the holes, and tie the string around your neck. Throughout the week, punch a hole in a group's card whenever you observe its members paying attention, following directions, volunteering, helping each other, or talking softly. At the end of the week, allow the group with the most holes in its card to choose prizes from a grab bag of treats. I keep the cards with me wherever we go. Students know that when my hole punch is in my "holster" and the cards are around my neck, I mean business!

Deena Block—Gr. 4
G. B. Fine Elementary
Pennsauken, NJ

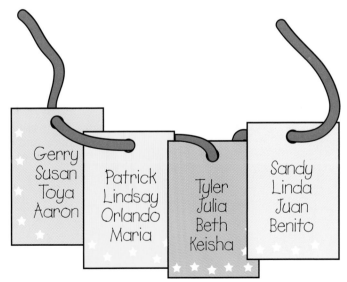

Free Time

Free-Time Reminders

If a student does not finish his work on time or misses a regular class assignment due to a pull-out program, have him write any unfinished assignment on a Post-it Brand note and attach it to his desk. This note serves as a free-time reminder to remind the student to make up his work during free time. If the work is still not completed during the day, have the student remove the Post-it note from his desk at the end of the day and attach it to his homework assignment sheet.

Ann Redmond—Gr. 4
Lower Salford Elementary
Harleysville, PA

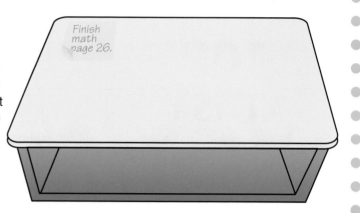

Paper-Free Center Activity

Providing free-time activities for intermediate students is a must, but they don't always have to be paper-and-pencil tasks. When your students are involved in a thematic study, place a related jigsaw puzzle at a center. Students can work on the puzzle during free time. When the puzzle is finished, take a photograph of students who worked on it; then display the photo in a Puzzle Photo Gallery in your classroom.

Wendy Rodda—Gr. 5, Lawrencetown Elementary, Lawrencetown, Nova Scotia, Canada

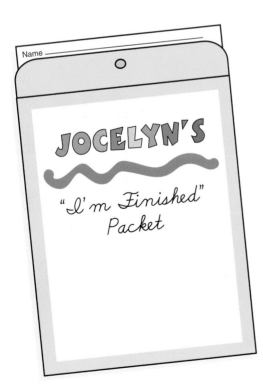

"I'm Finished" Packet

For those times when my students have completed classwork and need a break before beginning their homework, I prepare "I'm Finished" packets. For each student, I fill a large manila envelope with a variety of fun, independent activities—most of which I have found in back issues of *The Mailbox®* magazine and in *The Best of The Mailbox* books. The packets are kept at my desk when not in use. Students receive extra credit for every two completed activities. They enjoy working at their own pace and appreciate knowing that they have nothing to lose from their efforts.

Lynn Aydlett
Virginia Beach, VA

The Fix and Finish File

Free time is a great time to teach students to finish incomplete assignments and correct their own mistakes. Cover a box with colorful paper and label it "Fix and Finish File." Place a labeled file folder for each of your students in the box. If a student turns in work that needs to be finished or corrected, lightly highlight the area needing work and place the paper in the student's file. When a student has free time, he can take out his folder and get to work. What a great way to keep on top of things and eliminate idle time!

Karyn Tritelli—Gr. 4
St. Catherine of Siena School
Wilmington, DE

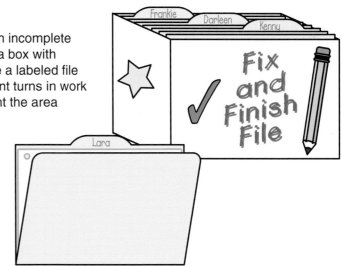

Extra Challenge "Enrichments"

To provide extra challenges for students who finish their work early, I've created a notebook full of "enrichments." This three-ring notebook is divided into categories such as math, research, creative ideas, art, and science. I make copies of reproducible pages from *The Mailbox®* magazine; then I punch holes in the pages and file them according to the categories. *The Mailbox* makes this job easy because the skill is printed in the upper right-hand corner of each reproducible. And each issue is filled with lots of enriching activities for my students! My enrichments notebook is available to all of my students. It challenges them to make use of extra time and gives them opportunities to choose their own activities.

Lea Iverson, Lincoln School, Elk River, MN

Extra-Credit Stickers

Want to keep early finishers from frittering away their extra time? At the start of each month, copy a supply of reproducible puzzles and skill sheets (one or more for each school day). Store the activities in a file box labeled "Extra Credit." Also make a chart listing each student's name and activity. If a student successfully completes an activity, write a check mark beside his name on the chart. At the end of the month, count the marks earned by each child, divide the total by two, and write the resulting quotient on a blank peel-off sticker. Give the sticker to the student; then let him affix it to a graded test and return the paper so you can add the extra-credit points to his final grade.

Adam Fassanella—Gr. 4
Hinsdale School
Winsted, CT

Homework and Classwork

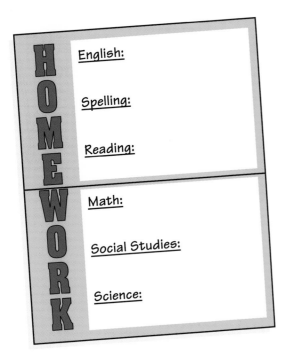

Assignment Board

Create more chalkboard space by posting daily assignments in another visible spot in the classroom. List the different subject areas on two poster board sheets. Laminate the sheets and post them on a small bulletin board adjacent to the chalkboard or on the side of a file cabinet. Add seasonal decorations if desired. Each day write the homework assignments on the sheets with a wipe-off marker.

Marilyn Davison—Grs. 4–5, River Oaks School, Monroe, LA

Do I Have Homework?

Tired of students rummaging through their desks trying to find their homework at the end of the day? Buy an inexpensive pocket folder for each student and write "Work Folder" and her name on the front. Place the folder on the student's desk and instruct her to leave it there all day. After completing a subject, have each student put her finished assignments in a folder in her desk. If an assignment is unfinished, have her put it inside her work folder. At the end of the day, a student can simply open her work folder to see if she has homework. If she does, it's right on her desk and ready to take home!

Doreen Placko—Gr. 5, St. Patrick School, Wadsworth, IL

Homework Calendar

Instead of assigning homework at the end of each day, I assign it on Monday for the entire week. To help my students plan ahead and complete their assignments by Friday's due date, I created a weekly homework calendar. I attached bulletin board border around a colorful sheet of poster board. Then I divided the board into four labeled sections as shown. Finally, I laminated the calendar. On Mondays I use an overhead marker to write each day's homework assignments on the board. Each student copies the assignments onto his own duplicated calendar (made to resemble the larger one). If a student has been absent, he can easily check the homework calendar when he returns to class. On Friday afternoons, I simply wipe the board clean so it's ready for Monday.

Bonnie Gibson—Gr. 5
Kyrene Monte Vista School
Tempe, AZ

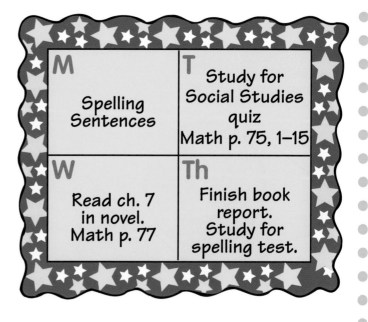

Assignment Pad Book Covers

Do your students take home their textbooks, but then forget what their assignments are? I have my students cover their texts with plain, brown grocery sacks. Each student draws a grid on the front and back of each cover, making a square for each school day of the month. The student then writes his daily assignment for that particular subject in the correct calendar box. At the beginning of each month, we make new covers for our books.

Lisa Borgo
Belleville, NJ

The Homework Stamp of Approval

Teaching students to keep a daily record of homework assignments is a small, but effective, way to teach responsibility. At the beginning of the year, have each student purchase a small notepad in which to write daily homework assignments. Encourage students to keep track of assignments as they're made by logging them in their pads. At the end of the day, select one student to stamp (using a seasonal rubber stamp) the pad of each classmate who has correctly listed all homework assignments for the night. To save your valuable time, check only a few students' pads each week; then reward each child who earned a stamp every day of the week with a small treat or class privilege.

Martha McDermott—Gr. 4, Camp Creek Elementary, Lilburn, GA

Cereal-Box Homework Caddies

Having a place to deposit assignments can really help the disorganized student stay on top of his work. Have each student bring an empty cereal box to school. Help students cut their boxes as shown; then provide glue and colorful paper so students can cover the boxes. Assign each child a number to write on the front of his box. Then staple the boxes together side by side. Each morning have students deposit homework assignments in their cereal-box caddies. As you check the boxes each morning, you'll notice in a snap, crackle, and pop who's come to school prepared!

Jennifer Kendt—Grs. 4–5
Ohio School
North Tonawanda, NY

Homework and Classwork

Homework Folder

Do your students have difficulty keeping track of homework? At the beginning of the school year, give each student a pocket folder labeled "Homework." Also give the student two labels: "To Do" and "Done." Have the student affix the "To Do" label to the left pocket and the other label to the right pocket. At the end of the day, have each child deposit assignments that need to be completed in the left pocket of his folder. At home, the student places completed homework in the right pocket. No more homework headaches!

Lisa Carlson
Bear Path Elementary
Hamden, CT

The "Due Today" Board

With a simple display, I give my more forgetful students the extra help they need to remember assignments. Near my homework assignment chart, I mount a small bulletin board titled "Due Today." Each morning I staple an extra copy of a homework assignment that is due that day to the board. Students can refer to this display whenever they need a reminder of work that is due.

Nancy Hatalsky—Gr. 4, Hiller Elementary, Madison Heights, MI

Assignment Signs

Instead of writing subject headings each day on your homework chalkboard, make these simple, movable signs. First, cut a colorful 3½" x 18" poster board strip for each subject you teach. Next, paste letters spelling the subject area (plus a picture if desired) on each strip. Laminate each strip and attach magnetic tape to its back. Arrange the subject signs on your chalkboard, allowing space for writing assignments. You can easily remove the signs for board washing, plus you can rearrange them to match your schedule.

Nancy Curl
Olson Middle School
Tabernacle, NJ

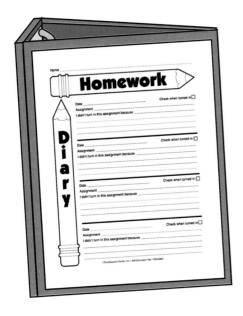

Homework Diary

Keep track of missed assignments—and emphasize students' responsibility to complete them—with the help of an inexpensive three-ring binder. Make a class supply of the form on page 168. Label a page for each student; then punch holes in the page and place it in the binder. When a student misses an assignment, have her fill out an entry on her binder page. Then, if a student or parent questions whether an assignment was turned in, you'll have an explanation of what happened in the student's own handwriting. Use the binder to monitor makeup work by checking the box on the form when the missing assignment is turned in.

Loraine Moore—Gr. 5, Pearl Prep School, Arcadia, CA

Goody Grab Bags

Three's the magic number when it comes to motivating my students! I fill three separate bags with an array of treats. In one bag, I place a variety of candy. I fill another bag with inexpensive items such as pencils, erasers, and notepads. The last bag is filled with homework passes and other special coupons. (See page 169.) When I want to recognize a student for exceptional effort, I let her "grab" a reward from the bag of her choice.

Theresa O'Connell—Gr. 5
Our Lady of Grace School
Greensboro, NC

Handy Homework Helper

Turn a bulletin board into a tool that keeps track of missing assignments and rewards students for responsible homework habits. For each student, cut the front from a manila file folder as shown. Staple the folder to a bulletin board along the sides to form a pocket; then label the folder with the student's name. Also make a supply of forms similar to the two shown on yellow and blue paper.

If a student is absent, place copies of the assignments he missed in his pocket. If a student owes you an assignment, fill out a yellow form and place it in his pocket to remind both him and you that he owes work. Slip a completed blue form into the pocket of any student who turned in all assignments for the week. How handy!

Carol Jorgensen
Lena Elementary
Lena, WI

Homework and Classwork

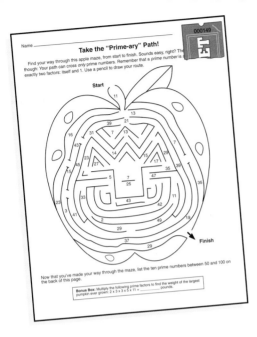

Motivating With Ticket Stubs

Looking for a way to motivate students to complete their homework? I tear inexpensive tickets in half; then I attach one ticket half to a homework assignment and place the other half in a fishbowl. As we check the assignment in class the next day, I periodically draw stubs from the fishbowl and call out the numbers. To be eligible for a prize, the student's homework must be complete and its ticket stub still attached. The activity is just the ticket for encouraging students to complete homework!

Merri Beth Bass—Gr. 4, Brookhill Elementary, Athens, AL

The Breakfast Club

Want to create in your students a hunger for doing their best? At the end of each month, reward students who have turned in all assignments and maintained responsible behavior by making them members of the Breakfast Club. One morning during the next month, invite this group of industrious students to join you 20 minutes before school for a delicious breakfast of doughnuts and juice.

Roseann Graf, Oak Ridge Elementary, Chino Hills, CA

One Smart Cookie

Responsibility, good work habits, cooperation—all are ingredients in one smart cookie! To encourage my students to be responsible, I post a chef cutout on a small bulletin board titled "What a Smart Cookie!" Also on the board, I place a student-generated list of "ingredients" for a smart cookie (see the example). At the end of the week, I name a student who exhibited these ingredients as the Smart Cookie of the Week. I write the student's name on a large cookie cutout and mount it on the board. In addition, I give the student a special certificate (see page 170) and a delicious cookie.

Lenore Kagan—Gr. 4
P.S. 150
Long Island City, NY

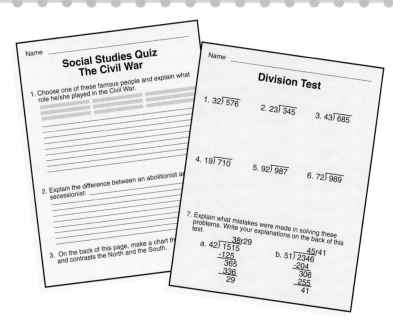

Colorful Tests

When duplicating tests, I run off two or three copies on colorful paper. On test day, I randomly distribute the tests; then I challenge students who get the colorful copies to make an A. I reward students who meet that challenge with a No Homework Pass. (See the pattern on page 169.) My students try harder to prepare for tests since they never know when they might receive a "colorful" copy.

Brenda N. Dalton
Cradock Middle School
Portsmouth, VA

Homework Motivation

Motivating students to turn in homework is easy with this sweet incentive. Each student writes her name in both upper corners of her paper before handing it in. Once I have recorded the grade, I cut off the left corner name and place it in a jar. Each Friday I draw one name from the jar. The winning child receives a piece of candy. Students soon realize that the more papers they hand in, the better their chances of winning.

Traci Baker—Gr. 4
Brassfield Elementary
Bixby, OK

For-Your-Best Stickers

Rather than place a sticker on every A and B paper, I found an alternative that my students actually prefer. I place a sticker on the one paper in the folder that represents the student's *best* effort. If a student is not capable of scoring an A or a B, she still gets a sticker for what is her best. It's a great way to tell a student that her best effort counts with me!

Beverly Langland—Gr. 5
Trinity Christian Academy
Jacksonville, FL

Stephanie
Math test

80

1. 3/8 of 24 = 9
2. 5/6 of 30 = 25
3. 2/3 of 15 = 10
4. 3/4 of 12 = 10
5. 4/5 of 15 = 12

Now We're Cooking!

Encourage a full class every day with this recipe for perfect attendance! On separate index cards, write each ingredient of a recipe for a special treat, such as chocolate chip cookies or muffins. For each day of perfect attendance, place one card in a bowl labeled "Now We're Cooking!" When all of the ingredients are in the bowl, cook or buy the class the tasty treat. Adapt this idea to reward other positive behaviors, such as homework completion or good behavior. If you don't want to use food as a reward, write words like *film, actors, director, screen, popcorn,* and *projector* on the cards for a fun movie reward. What a terrific way to let students know what special ingredients they are in your class!

Kimberly Minafo—Gr. 4
Tooker Avenue School
West Babylon, NY

Late Work Solution

To keep late work at a minimum, I set monthly goals for my class. For example, the class goal for September may be to have less than 25 late assignments (that's only one late assignment per child). If we meet our goal, the class will have a popcorn party; then a new goal is set for the following month. I try to raise the standards a little each month. The students' sense of responsibility is increased—especially when they see the impact it can have on others.

Joan E. Fate—Gr. 4, Whittier School, Clinton, IA

Stickers That Stick Around

Are you tired of seeing special stickers that you've purchased to put on students' papers stuffed in desks or in the garbage? To make the stickers and returned work more meaningful to students, try using sticker boards. Cut a 4" x 10" piece of oaktag for each student. Write each student's name on a different piece of oaktag. Instead of placing stickers directly on their work, pass out the sticker boards and stickers. Stress to the students that the boards are collections of stickers—not a competition. I keep the sticker boards on my desk for safekeeping and laminate them when they are filled with stickers. Then I get another one ready immediately for each child. My students love the stickers that really "stick around"!

Elise Nash—Gr. 5, Delaware Academy
Delhi, NY

Student-of-the-Day Bookmarks

Encourage attendance with the help of a Student-of-the-Day calendar. Make a supply of the award bookmarks found on page 169. Cut out the bookmarks and store them in a basket. At the start of each month, write a student's name and an interesting historical fact or famous person's birthday in each school day on a large calendar. Explain to the class that the child whose name is listed in a particular space will be that day's honored student.

Each morning have the student of the day read his fact to the class. During the day, allow the honored child to run errands and perform special tasks for you. As a thank-you gift, let him pick a bookmark from the basket. Not only does the student earn extra strokes for being helpful, but he also has a special class privilege to look forward to.

Therese Durhman—Gr. 5, Mountain View School, Hickory, NC

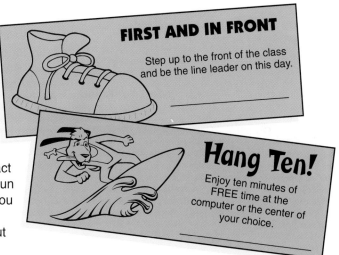

FIRST AND IN FRONT
Step up to the front of the class and be the line leader on this day.

Hang Ten!
Enjoy ten minutes of FREE time at the computer or the center of your choice.

100% Homework Club

What do I do to combat the problem of incomplete homework assignments? I formed a 100% Homework Club. To be eligible for membership, a student must turn in all of his assignments and promptly return papers that need to be signed. If a student succeeds for an entire month, he becomes a member of the club for the following month. Club members are treated to a party, receive special certificates, and enjoy the privilege of using special coat and bookbag hooks for the month. Now over half of my 29 students routinely make the club each month. Even students who don't make the club have fewer late homework assignments. This idea is so popular that other fourth and fifth grades at our school have started their own 100% Homework Clubs.

Jack M. Dibee Jr.—Gr. 4, Lincoln Grade School, Murphysboro, IL

REDEEMABLE IN MS. NOVAK'S CLASS

HOMEWORK TICKET

ONE TICKET

Homework Teams

When even one student doesn't bring in a homework assignment, the paperwork that irresponsibility creates can add up. To cut down on missing homework, I organize my class into four teams. Each morning students give their homework to a selected teammate, who organizes all of the papers according to subject. If all members of a team bring in their homework, that team is rewarded with a homework ticket. Five tickets earn a team the opportunity to select an award from a posted list of special privileges (generated by students and approved by me). This method means I no longer have to shuffle through several stacks of papers each day or keep track of as many late assignments. Plus the pressure to do homework has shifted from me to the students.

Patricia Novak—Gr. 4, Meadowbrook School, Eatontown, NJ

"Berry" Good Spellers

Motivate your students to prepare for spelling tests with a "berry" easy idea! Make a class supply of the berry pattern on page 170. Have students color and cut out their berries; then have them store the cutouts in personal work folders. When a child scores 100 percent on a spelling test, use a hole puncher to punch out one of the numbers on her berry. After all ten numbers have been punched, reward the student with a No Homework Pass (see the pattern on page 169); then give her another pattern so that she can continue this "berry" motivating project.

Betty Wastlick—Gr. 4
St. Mary's School
Richland Center, WI

Clean Desk Fairy

When classroom desks need tidying up a bit, try this variation of the clean desk fairy. A few minutes before the morning bell rings, sprinkle gold glitter and leave pieces of sugarless candy on the top of several clean desks. The students will be ecstatic to find the magical fairy dust and candy on their clean desks. And their classmates will be motivated to work harder to keep their areas clean too.

Rebecca J. Hindman—Gr. 4, Joshua Intermediate School, Burleson, TX

Take-Home Project Kits

Unfortunately, some students dread homework projects because their families can't afford or don't provide supplies. Take-home project kits solve this problem! To make a kit, fill a large plastic storage bag with basic supplies, such as markers, a glue stick, a ruler, a pair of child-safe scissors, a box of crayons, and several sheets of 9" x 12" construction paper. Make about five or six kits available for students to check out for two to three days at a time. Now every child will have the tools she needs to create a great project!

Lisa Staub
Columbia, MD

Motivational Moolah

Here's an idea that is especially effective during the last quarter of the school year when motivation is likely to hit an all-time low. Make a supply of "motivational moolah" bills (see the pattern on page 171). Announce to students that they will be able to earn the money for such behaviors as turning in assignments on time, keeping desks tidy, following class rules, and completing extra-credit work. Conversely, they will be fined for breaking class rules, not turning in work, and exhibiting irresponsible behavior. Mount a poster listing ways to earn money and fines (see the example). Have each student make a simple ledger in which to record his earnings and fines. Allow students to use their money to buy class privileges such as extra computer or recess time. Or encourage them to save their bucks to spend at an end-of-the-year "white elephant" auction, stocked with items donated by students and their families.

Eileen J. Harford—Grs. 5 & 6
Orchard Middle School
Solon, OH

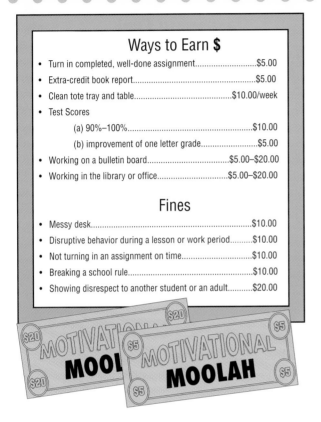

Ways to Earn $

- Turn in completed, well-done assignment..........................$5.00
- Extra-credit book report..$5.00
- Clean tote tray and table...$10.00/week
- Test Scores
    (a) 90%–100%..$10.00
    (b) improvement of one letter grade.........................$5.00
- Working on a bulletin board...................................$5.00–$20.00
- Working in the library or office...............................$5.00–$20.00

Fines

- Messy desk...$10.00
- Disruptive behavior during a lesson or work period..........$10.00
- Not turning in an assignment on time.............................$10.00
- Breaking a school rule..$10.00
- Showing disrespect to another student or an adult..........$20.00

Paper Toppers

Searching for a way to motivate students to turn in neat, legible assignments? Periodically tape a novelty pencil to the top of each neatly done assignment. Students will be thrilled to receive this reward even though their work may contain mistakes. Top that!

Patricia E. Dancho, Apollo-Ridge Middle School, Spring Church, PA

Homework Moviefest

Motivate students to complete homework assignments with this silver screen incentive. At the start of each month, label a blank calendar page for each child. During the month, place a sticker on each day that a student turns in all homework assignments (and also on any day he is absent). At the end of the month, give each student who received a sticker every day a no-homework pass and an invitation to a special "moviefest." Also send invitations—without the homework passes—to students who have only one or two no-sticker days. During the moviefest, show a curriculum-related video and serve popcorn or other refreshments.

Kelly Fornauf—Gr. 5
Northwestern Lehigh Middle School
New Tripoli, PA

GOOD FOR YOU!
You're invited to December's moviefest!

Listening Dial

Motivate your students to tune in to your lessons with a Listening Dial. First, model what it means to be a good listener by using the acronym LISTEN: Look at the speaker, Interact in discussion, Sit up straight, Think, Enjoy, No interrupting. Then create a Listening Dial (see the illustration) to let your students know just how well they are listening each day. When the class is displaying good listening skills, place the dial on the character with a wide smile and big ears. When the students need to improve their listening skills, warn them by moving the dial to the character with smaller ears. If the listening improves, move the dial back to its original position.

Joan E. Fate—Gr. 4
Whittier Elementary
Clinton, IA

Homework Motivator

To encourage students to complete their homework, fill a small trunk with inexpensive treats; then close and padlock the trunk. Place the padlock's key on a ring with two similar keys. Duplicate the homework incentive chart on page 172 for each student. Also make a supply of the key pattern on page 172.

After checking homework, stamp one space on the chart of each student who completed his assignment. When the last box on a row is stamped, give the child a No Homework Pass (see the pattern on page 169) and a paper key. On Friday, let each student who earned a paper key choose one key from the ring and try to open the padlock. If he picks the right key, allow the lucky student to select a treat from inside the trunk.

Linda Eller—Gr. 6, Idlewild Elementary, Memphis, TN

Gumball Rewards

I keep a gumball machine on my desk and lots of extra pennies in a drawer. When a student completes an extra-credit activity, scores well on an assignment, or earns a special treat, I give her a laminated gumball machine award. The award can be turned in at the end of the day for two pennies, which in turn can be used in the gumball machine. Students love this colorful treat and so do I. It's very inexpensive to buy gumballs, and the awards can be recycled. I also tape pennies right on students' papers. It's amazing what children will do to earn a couple of pennies!

Julie Carty—Gr. 4
Dysart-Geneseo Elementary
Dysart, IA

Whale of an Incentive Program

Make a big splash with this classroom incentive program! Use a die-cutter to create a supply of whale cutouts. Each time a student exhibits exemplary behavior or work habits, present him with a cutout to recognize a whale of a good job. Direct students to sign the whales they receive and store them in a safe place. Throughout the year, ask parents to donate small incentives, such as bookmarks, magnets, stickers, and used books. Then periodically hold an auction during which students use their collected whales to buy the assorted donations.

Anne Nichol—Gr. 4
West Madison Elementary
Madison, AL

Classroom Jobs

Motivate your students to complete their work by offering special jobs for those who finish early. On the board list jobs such as watering plants, dusting shelves, and straightening book displays. When a student finishes her work, have her check with you for approval. Then have the student choose a job to do. When she has completed the job, ask her to erase it from the board. Not only does this offer an incentive to your students, it also helps keep your classroom in tip-top shape.

Mary Dinneen
Mountain View School
Bristol, CT

Perfect Paper Punch Cards

For a practically perfect way to motivate good work habits, cut off the front of a greeting card for each student. Draw ten to 15 dots on the card with a marker; then give the card to a student. Each time the student earns a perfect score, punch out one dot on her card. When all dots have been punched, reward the child with a small treat. Then give her another card. At the end of the grading period, award a prize to each student who turns in all of the completely punched cards she earned during that period of weeks.

Kris Call—Gr. 5
St. Joseph School
Decatur, IN

Happy
Birthday
to You!

Homework and Classwork

Give It Your Best Shot!

Need a simple, inexpensive way to motivate and reward students? How about letting them shoot some hoops! I mount a plastic basketball hoop over a bulletin board in my classroom. Whenever a student answers a question correctly, makes an extra effort to participate in class, or needs recognition in some way, I allow him to take a shot at the hoop with a small soft basketball. The ball and goal are never used for physical education or free time, so students really look forward to the privilege of taking shots. It's a great way to review for tests, reward an individual for a thoughtful deed, or just add some fun to the day.

Pamela C. Broome—Gr. 5, Rockwell Elementary, Rockwell, NC

Class Test Average

In my class, tests aren't a dreaded evil, but a fun class challenge! Each time my students take a test, they try to work together to beat our previous class test average. This challenge encourages my students to work harder on their individual scores in order to bring up the class average. When we beat our average, everyone has a reason to celebrate!

Roseann Graf, Oak Ridge Elementary, Chino Hills, CA

Handy Homework Tip

If you teach in a departmentalized setting, try this handy tip for helping students take responsibility for homework. Divide a large piece of poster board according to the number of periods you teach (see the illustration). Each time every student in class turns in his homework, add a letter in *homework* to the chart as shown. When a class finally spells *homework,* treat it to a popcorn and video party. With this tip, students put the pressure to do homework on each other, so you don't have to!

Monica Moss—Special Education Grs. 5–8
Iuka, MS

1st: H
2nd: HOM
3rd: HOME
5th: HO
6th: HOMEW
7th: HOMEWORK

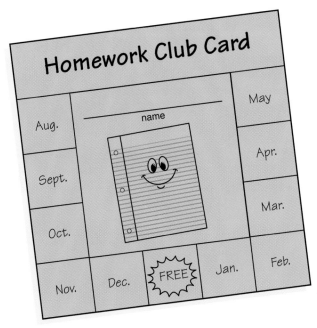

Homework Club Card

Want to increase students' motivation for doing homework? Then join the club—the Homework Club, that is! Make a class supply of the Homework Club Card pattern on page 173. Explain to the class that you understand that circumstances occasionally make it difficult to complete homework. Then distribute the homework cards, each of which entitles its owner to one free homework pass per month, plus one additional "FREE" space to use any month. When a student wants to use a pass, he brings the card to you; then you punch a hole in the appropriate month's space (or the "FREE" space). In the beginning, students will probably rush to use the cards right away. But gradually they'll learn the advantages of saving the pass for emergencies, such as when an assignment is accidentally left at home or forgotten.

Joy Allen & Marcia Crouch—Gr. 4
Sam Houston Elementary
Bryan, TX

Auction Coupons

What intermediate kid wasn't born to shop? With that fact in mind, I motivate my students by holding an auction every other month. I begin by making and cutting out a supply of small coupons. On Friday, I give a coupon to each student who has exhibited good effort and behavior during the week. Students store their coupons in envelopes. About four or five times a year, I hold an auction during which students can spend their coupons on baked goods (donated by parents) and other inexpensive items.

Nancy Murphy—Gr. 5, Converse School, Beloit, WI

HOT Tickets

When spring fever hits—or a big holiday is approaching—minds turn anywhere but to homework! Increase the motivation to complete homework with this simple solution. Make copies of the "HOT Ticket" (Homework on Time) pattern on page 173 on orange paper. Each time a student completes his homework and turns it in on time, let him fill out a ticket and place it in a special container. At the end of the week, draw one or more tickets; then award a special prize to each lucky winner. Want to work a little math practice into this incentive? On Friday morning, announce the number of tickets in the container; then have each student determine the probability of his name being drawn, based on the number of tickets he earned during the week.

Joy Allen & Marcia Crouch—Gr. 4

Homework and Classwork

Homework Bucket

Teachers aren't the only ones who need a helping hand where homework is concerned—parents do too! In a letter sent home at the beginning of the year, suggest to parents that they fill an inexpensive bucket, plastic bin, or basket with the following items: special homework pencils and pens, a stapler, paper clips, colored pencils, page markers, sticky notes, highlighters, and any other office supplies that the child might like. Have the parents stipulate that the supplies can *only* be used for completing homework. Students will love having their own "offices" to work from at home.

Janet Bavonese—Gr. 4
Perrine Baptist Academy
Miami, FL

Paper of the Day

Encourage students to carefully complete their work with this paper-of-the-day plan. Conclude each day by presenting one outstanding assignment that was completed that day. Enlist your students' help in identifying the positive qualities of the paper such as neatness, accuracy, originality, and completeness. Then showcase the paper in a special frame designed for this purpose. A round of applause for the proud owner of the paper of the day is definitely in order!

Debbie Byrne
Candor Elementary, Candor, NY

Hooray for Homework!

Students who shout "Hooray for homework"? It could happen with this monthly motivator. At the end of each month, hold an awards ceremony to honor students who turned in all of their homework assignments. Present each deserving student with a special certificate that entitles her to skip homework one night during the upcoming month. Did someone just say "Hooray"?

Kirsten Sasaki
Copiague Middle School
Copiague, NY

Accordion File to the Rescue!

Most of my students keep a separate folder for each subject. Invariably, a more disorganized child brings the wrong folder to class, leaving the correct one in her homeroom. Or she frequently files a paper in the wrong folder. To help, I ask the child's parents to purchase a letter-size accordion file with about eight to ten sections. I label each section with a different subject, in the order of the student's class schedule. Now the child can store all of her papers in one convenient place, with only *one* file to keep up with. Even some of my organized students have started using this tip!

Terry Castoria—Gr. 5, Frank Defino Central School, Marlboro, NJ

Assignment Board

No more "Do we have any homework?" with this handy assignment board! Each month I draw a calendar grid on a sheet of poster board. I display the calendar on a bulletin board along with a fine-tipped marker. Each week a student helper records all daily work on the calendar. In addition, each student has a notebook in which he records the assignments. Students who are absent can check the board when they return to school. I save each calendar; then, at the end of the year, I show my amazed students all the work they have accomplished.

Julie Kwoka—Gr. 5, George Southard Elementary, Lockport, NY

Color-Coded Handouts

"Where do I put this?" Yes, it's the desperate call of the disorganized student! At the start of the new school year, display a poster as shown. Throughout the year, copy all handouts on paper that coordinates with the poster's color code (for example, duplicate all math sheets on green paper, all language handouts on blue paper, etc.). When a student receives a handout, he'll know to file it in his notebook with other papers of that color. Toward the end of the school year, start duplicating all handouts on white paper (with the appropriate subject noted at the top) to get students ready for the increased responsibilities of the next grade level.

Liane Kabatoff—Gr. 5
Lochearn School
Rocky Mountain House, Alberta, Canada

Color Us Organized!

= English

= Writing

= Reading

= Math

= Science and Health

= Social Studies

Student Organization

Helping Students Get Organized

One method I use for helping students with their organizational skills is to have each child make classwork and take-home folders. When a student completes a daily assignment, he puts it in his classwork folder—instead of shoving it inside a textbook never to be found again. When we check work the next day, the student can take his classwork folder from his desk and easily find his paper. At the end of the day, students place incomplete assignments to finish for homework, handouts, assignment sheets, memos, and other important information into their take-home folders; then they put these folders into their backpacks to take home. This easy system certainly has reduced the number of "I forgot" and "I lost it" excuses!

Pamela J. Fox—Gr. 4
Brassfield Elementary
Bixby, OK

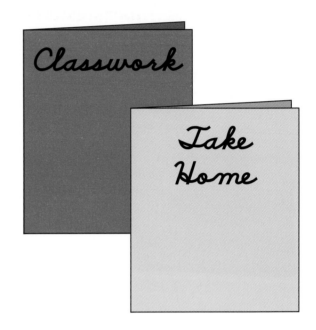

Table Crates

Plastic file-holding crates make wonderful caddies for student work and supplies. Provide each cooperative group with one crate and a hanging file folder for each student in the group. Inside her folder the student stores her work-in-progress folder, journal, and portfolio. In addition, place a cup and small box inside each crate to hold pencils, rulers, etc. Every Friday afternoon students choose items from their work-in-progress folders to place in their portfolios. This system provides students with easy access to their work and enhances their organizational skills.

Christy Pine—Gr. 5
Wilson Elementary
Riverside, CA

Graded-Papers Notebook

Dreaming of a way to keep graded work from becoming an organizational nightmare? Each of my students has a binder notebook with a labeled divider for each subject. In the front of each subject section, the student keeps a table of contents page (see the illustration). I hole-punch three holes in all graded papers before distributing them. Each student places her papers in the correct sections of her notebook. She then lists each assignment and its grade in the appropriate table of contents. When it's time to study for a test, the student has all of her graded work at her fingertips. She also has a list of her grades, so there's never a surprise when report card time rolls around. Each student takes her notebook home—along with a parent signature form—each Friday for parents to see.

Shannon Hillis—Gr. 5, La Maddalena American School, Italy

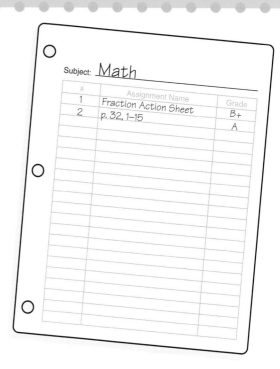

Subject: Math

#	Assignment Name	Grade
1	Fraction Action Sheet	B+
2	p. 32, 1–15	A

Saving Papers for Quizzes

To motivate my students to stay organized, I give each child a special folder for each new unit. All papers and assignments for that unit are kept in the folder. At the end of the unit, each student is allowed to use the papers in his folder as a reference during the final test. If a student has carefully filed papers in his folder, he earns this special advantage during testing. Motivation made simple!

Phyllis Ellett—Grs. 3–4 Multiage, Earl Hanson Elementary, Rock Island, IL

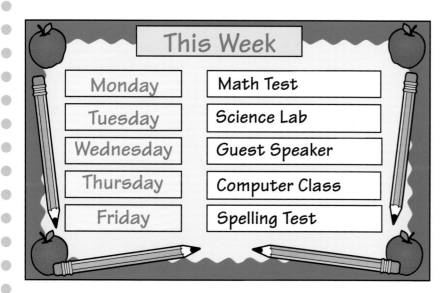

This Week

Monday	Math Test
Tuesday	Science Lab
Wednesday	Guest Speaker
Thursday	Computer Class
Friday	Spelling Test

This Week

Keep your students informed of the week's upcoming events with this timely idea. Label five strips of paper with the days of the week and attach them to a small bulletin board or wall space. Next to each day, use a similar strip of paper to list the day's highlight, such as "Math Test" or "Computer Class." Update the highlights each Monday. Add a seasonal border and holiday decorations each month for a display that makes everyone aware of the week's main events!

Dawn Livengood—Gr. 5,
Wilson Intermediate School
Pekin, IL

Student Organization

Remember!

REMEMBER!

Tues. 3-9: Science test

Wed. 3-10: Money for field trip

Fri. 3-12: Hand in book report

Remember!

To help students become more responsible for remembering important due dates, label a corner of the chalkboard "Remember!" In this space, list any upcoming event—but *only* if a student asks you to list the item. Then review the list at the end of the day. Students will quickly realize how helpful it is to have the reminders right in front of them. If desired, discontinue the "Remember!" list during the last quarter of the school year, and encourage each student to keep her own list at her desk.

Gratsiela Sabangan—Grs. 4–6, Three Angels School Wichita, KS

Grade Tracking

Intermediate students are very grade conscious; yet most would say that it's the teacher's—not the student's—responsibility to keep track of grades. Not so in my classroom! To help my students learn how to keep track of their own grades, I give each child a blank grade sheet form. Each time I return a graded paper to students, I remind them to log it onto their grade sheets. If a student's grade sheet is correctly completed at the end of a six-week period, I reward the child with bonus points in the subject of his choice. Not only do students learn responsibility as they track their grades, but they also communicate their progress to their parents more frequently—an added bonus for me!

Betsy Fannin—Gr. 5, Bloom Middle School, South Webster, OH

Assignment Folders With a Twist

Looking for a way to organize each student's graded assignments? Try this system that also involves students in valuable critical thinking about their work. Label an assignment folder for each child; then place seven colorful sheets of paper in each folder, labeled as follows:

- Best Work
- Assignment That Allowed Personal Expression
- Most Difficult Assignment
- Most Enjoyable Assignment
- Least Difficult Assignment
- Most Creative Assignment
- Assignment That Taught Me the Most

Give each child another folder to keep in his desk for storing graded work. Every few weeks have each student choose a paper from his desk folder to put behind each of the labeled sheets in his assignment folder, replacing older papers as desired. This system teaches students to keep up with graded work and critically evaluate their assignments. Plus it's a great tool for parent-teacher conferences.

Linda Flores, Melanie Haynes, and Sandra Tilford
Southwest RV Elementary, Washburn, MO

Too Many Interruptions?

Do you encourage your students to go to each other with questions before coming to you? Then it's likely that sometimes your helping students are interrupted so frequently that they struggle to get their own work done. To curb this problem, duplicate the patterns on page 174 on bright yellow paper (one copy for every three students). Have each student cut out a smiley pattern and "Shhh!" pattern and glue them back-to-back onto a tongue depressor as shown. Attach a piece of magnetic tape to each side of the depressor so it will stick to the side of a student's desk. If a student is open to questions, he displays the smiling face. But if he doesn't want to be distracted from his work, he displays the "Shhh!" face to gently signal classmates not to interrupt him for a while. Try using one of these management tools yourself the next time you need a little quiet time too!

Barbara Wilkes Delnero—Gr. 4
Tuckerton Elementary
Tuckerton, NJ

Personal Helper

To help a child who's having difficulty with organization, I ask a classmate to be his personal helper. The helper reminds the child of classwork assigned while he was out of the room for a pull-out activity. He also makes sure that his charge has packed all necessary books and assignments in his bookbag at the end of the day. After about six weeks, the disorganized student usually no longer needs help. I thank the helper with an inexpensive gift.

Vera Stillman, Menlo Park School, Edison, NJ

Is It Done Yet?

Help your students evaluate their projects before turning them in with this idea. When a project is first assigned, give students the requirements and criteria that will be used to grade it. Then share the following acronym to help students know when their projects are done: Details, Originality, Neatness, Editing. Provide each student with a copy of the checklist on page 175. Discuss each term so that the student knows exactly what is expected of him. Before turning in his final project, have the child complete the checklist and attach it to his project. With this easy-to-use form, students will gain important insight about the qualities of a good finished project.

Meg Turner
Durham, NC

Is It Done Yet?
How do you know if your project is done? Use the checklist below as a guide.

Details
☐ Have you included all text necessary for understanding?
☐ Have you used illustrations to add to your project?
☐ Are your illustrations colorful?

Originality
☐ Have you written the text in your own words?
☐ Have you used your own creative design?

Neatness
☐ Is your final copy written in ink or typed?
☐ Have all pencil marks been completely erased?

Editing
☐ Are all words spelled correctly?
☐ Have all capitalization rules been followed?
☐ Have all punctuation rules been followed?
☐ Have you checked for correct grammar?

Comments_____
_____
_____

Name _____ Date _____

Student Organization

Have Binder, Will Travel!

A three-ring binder = an organizational lifesaver? It does in my class! Each of my students has a two-inch binder that holds these items:

- a pocket folder (labeled "Home Folder") for storing notes to parents and completed homework
- an assignment notebook
- a spiral notebook
- notebook paper
- a pencil case containing two pencils, a red pen, and a highlighter

No matter where my students are, they're always prepared. Have binder, will travel!

Pat Murray—Grs. 3–4
St. Rita of Cascia School
Aurora, IL

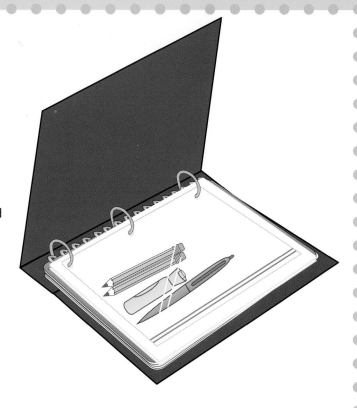

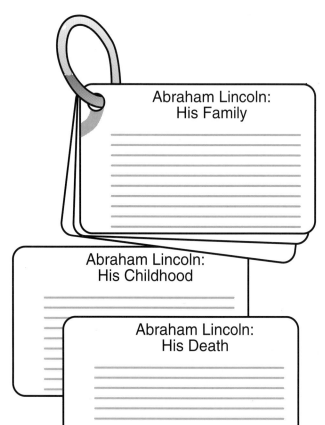

Hanging On to Notecards

Do your students often misplace their notecards—right before an assigned paper is due? Is it confusing for them to keep their notecards in order? One solution is for each student to label 4" x 6" notecards with the subject she is researching. After punching a hole in the upper left-hand corner of each card, have the student insert a metal ring through the entire set. She can then fasten the ring in her notebook or on a hook in her cubby, or keep it in her writing folder. With this handy tip, students will easily be able to keep all their information together.

Margaret C. Howell—Librarian
West Springfield Elementary
Fairfax County, VA

Color-Coded Notebooks

Have you ever discovered a student's math work in his reading journal? Or his journal writing in his math journal? To help students readily recognize and use the appropriate spiral notebook, try this color-coded tab system. Laminate several sheets of construction paper, one color for each subject-area notebook that your students use. Cut the sheets into 3 cm x 23 cm strips and give each student one strip of each color. Direct the student to tape each strip to the inside cover of the corresponding notebook, leaving about 2 cm extending above the top. Then, at the front of the classroom, post large paper strips in the same colors labeled with the matching subjects. When it's time to use a notebook, students can easily identify the right one!

Julie VandeBerg—Gr. 4
Rosendale Intermediate School
Brandon, WI

Magnetic Management

Here's a really "attractive" way to help students who, no matter how hard they try, consistently misplace their worksheets. Use refrigerator magnets to hang an extra worksheet from a filing cabinet. When a student loses a reproducible, let him copy (but not remove) the hanging sheet. You won't have to scramble to make an extra copy, and the student gets a chance to make up his work.

Judith Brinckerhoff, Hanaford School, East Greenwich, RI

Flashy Folders

Looking for a plan that will help students organize handouts and graded papers in a flash? For each subject, provide every student with a different-colored folder (one with brads), coordinating the folder colors with those of your textbooks. Also provide a folder for homework. Have each student label each folder with its subject; then have her store her folders in a labeled magazine box that is kept on a bookshelf in the classroom. Before distributing handouts to students, hole-punch them so students can file them in the appropriate folders. At the end of the day, have students take any folders out of their desks and return them to their magazine boxes. Send the homework folders home. Organized students in a flash!

Michelle R. Pratt—Gr. 4, James Morris School, Morris, CT, and
Melaine Brown, Western Middle School, Elon College, NC

Student Organization

Daily Checklist

Do you live and die by your "To Do" list? To help my students learn to use this handy organizational tool, I attach a checklist to each child's desk with clear adhesive paper. (Use the reproducible on page 176 to create a checklist for your class.) The list reminds students of all the tasks they must do during our class's opening period and closing period each day. During each of these times, each student must go down the checklist and put an imaginary check next to each completed task on the list. The responsibility for remembering these daily tasks is now on the shoulders of my students, not mine.

Loraine Moore—Gr. 4, Pearl Preparatory School, El Monte, CA

Partner Up!

Here's a simple way to make sure even your most disorganized students don't miss important information. Divide the class into pairs, placing each student who struggles with organizational skills with a capable classmate. Write the following responsibilities on the board and discuss them with the class:

- Check my partner's assignment pad at the end of the day. Initial the sheet to verify that it is correct.
- Make my partner aware of assignments or announcements he may have missed if absent from the class for any reason.

At the end of several weeks, hold a "Partner Powwow" during which students share about the partnering experience. Then assign new pairs and let the partnerships begin!

Faye K. Wells, Marion City Elementary, Buena Vista, GA

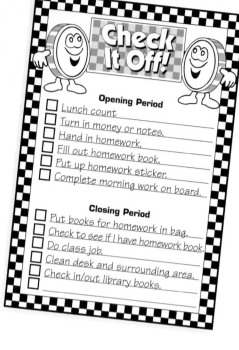

Clip It!

Add a clipboard to your students' supply list for a management system that's hard to beat! Each Monday I give students new assignment sheets, which they clip to their clipboards. They also turn in the preceding week's sheets that I send home with their work packets so that parents can see how completely assignments are being recorded.

During the day as they change classes, students take their clipboards with them. They record their daily assignments, plus attach reproducibles and take-home notes. (This is a good way to keep loose papers from being stuffed in a book or backpack, never to be found again!) Students get the hang of this system quickly and remember to take their clipboards home daily. And parents always know where to look for their children's assignments and notes from school.

Marilyn Davison—Grs. 4 & 5, River Oaks School, Monroe, LA

Three Cheers for Checklists

Getting students to return daily assignment checklists to school was often frustrating for me. Students were always misplacing or losing the single sheets. To solve the problem, I started compiling enough daily checklists for a month into an attractive booklet for each student. Each checklist features a place for a parent signature, nightly assignments, and a note from the teacher. Students are able to keep a record of their monthly progress with the booklets and are less likely to lose them. Best of all, the booklets keep parents informed of their children's progress on a daily basis.

S. Beth Murphy—Gr. 4
Memorial Elementary
Jackson, MI

Managing Writing Assignments

Frustrated by the stacks of creative-writing papers facing me, I decided to make my students more responsible for their work. First, I made a writing portfolio for each child. Each week I place two or three completed (and dated) writing assignments in each student's folder. At the end of three weeks, I give the child his portfolio with instructions to read his papers for continuity, creative ability, and mechanics. Next, I have each student choose one paper for a peer to edit. After the editing stage, each student corrects or rewrites his paper; then he attaches to it a paragraph describing his writing weaknesses and strengths. Students submit their papers and paragraphs to me, and we discuss them during individual conferences. This system has made my kids much more responsible students and writers.

Pam Williams—Gr. 4, Dixieland Elementary, Lakeland, FL

Tube Tote

To ensure that maps, posters, and other large projects make it home and back to school in good condition, have each student bring in an empty paper towel tube to decorate with her own personal designs. Oversized papers can be rolled up and placed in the tube for safe transport. These tubes fit easily into backpacks and can be stored in student mailboxes or desks until the next time they are needed.

Paul La Belle—Gr. 4, George H. Potter School, New Bedford, MA

Check Your Flags

To help my students remember upcoming test dates, I attach test flags to my daily assignment board. Constructed from red construction paper, each small triangle is laminated and backed with a magnet. When a test is announced, a student abbreviates the test date on the flag with a dry-erase pen and places it on the board by the subject. Students enjoy programming the flags and "flying" them for their classmates. At the end of each day, I remind my students to "check your flags." These flags can be cleaned and reprogrammed throughout the year.

Debra Hess—Gr. 5
St. Augustine School
Kelso, MO

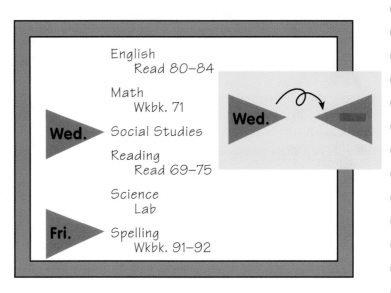

Unit Folders

Give students' organizational skills and test scores a boost with this fantastic folder idea. First, have each student decorate a folder in which to store all work related to a specific unit. At the end of the unit, post a sequential list of the notes, handouts, and assignments each student should have in his folder. After students check their folders by the list, collect and grade them according to their level of organization. Give extra points to students whose folders are complete. Then, as the school year progresses, watch as test scores climb higher because students spend their time studying instead of looking for lost papers!

Sue Hadden—Gr. 5
Hylen Souders Elementary
Galena, OH

Clip It!

My students are always misplacing their journals. To help them keep up with these important booklets, I alphabetized my class list and assigned a number to each student. I wrote each student's number on a pinch clothespin; then I used double-sided tape to attach each clothespin along a classroom wall. Now when it's time for students to go home, they simply clip their booklets to their clothespins. At a glance, I can quickly see who has forgotten to turn in his journal.

Jane Richardson—Gr. 4
Taylor Mill Elementary
Covington, KY

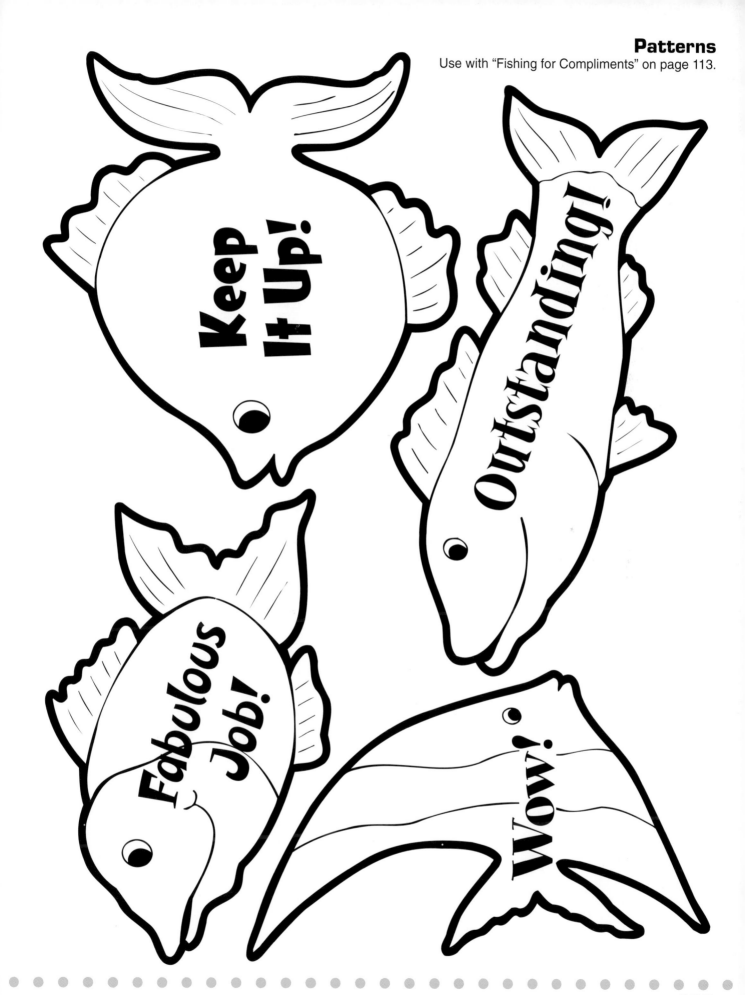

Keep It Up!

Outstanding!

Fabulous Job!

Wow!

Patterns

Use with "Cooldown Cards" on page 121.

COOL-DOWN CARD

What's the problem?

What can I do to correct the problem?

Why shouldn't I be exhibiting this behavior?

_____   Student

Teacher/Date   Parent
(Please sign and return.)

©The Education Center, Inc. • *500 Classroom Tips* • TEC60849

COOL-DOWN CARD

What's the problem?

What can I do to correct the problem?

Why shouldn't I be exhibiting this behavior?

_____   Student

Teacher/Date   Parent
(Please sign and return.)

©The Education Center, Inc. • *500 Classroom Tips* • TEC60849

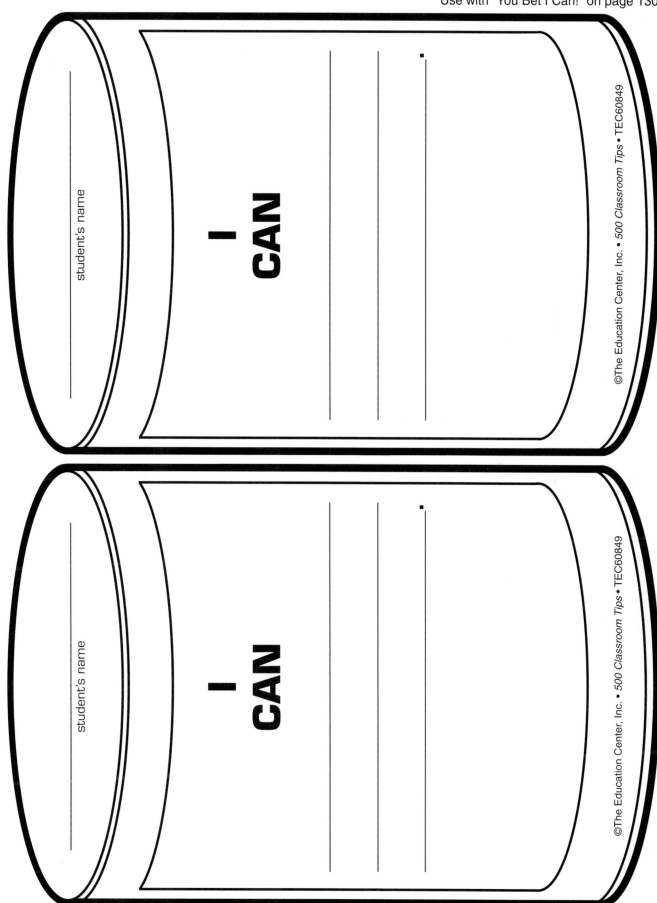

student's name

I CAN

©The Education Center, Inc. • *500 Classroom Tips* • TEC60849

student's name

I CAN

©The Education Center, Inc. • *500 Classroom Tips* • TEC60849

Cloud Patterns
Use with "The Sky's the Limit!" on page 131.

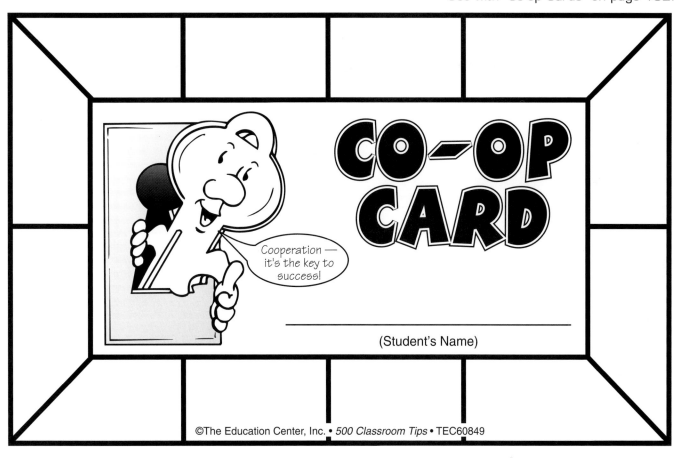

©The Education Center, Inc. • *500 Classroom Tips* • TEC60849

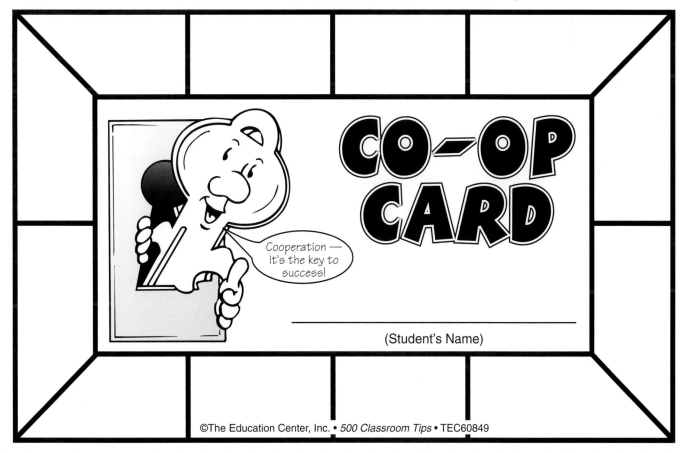

©The Education Center, Inc. • *500 Classroom Tips* • TEC60849

Name _____

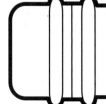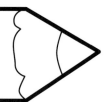

Homework

Date _____   Check when turned in ☐

Assignment _____

I didn't turn in this assignment because _____

_____

_____

_____

Date _____   Check when turned in ☐

Assignment _____

I didn't turn in this assignment because _____

_____

_____

_____

Date _____   Check when turned in ☐

Assignment _____

I didn't turn in this assignment because _____

_____

_____

_____

Date _____   Check when turned in ☐

Assignment _____

I didn't turn in this assignment because _____

_____

_____

Diary

Note to the teacher: Use with "Homework Diary" on page 141.

Use with "Goody Grab Gags" on page 141 and "Student-of-the-Day Bookmarks" on page 145. Also use the No Homework Pass with "Colorful Tests" on page 143, "'Berry' Good Spellers" on page 146, and "Homework Motivator" on page 148.

NO HOMEWORK PASS

Assignment:

_____

name

Munch With Me!

For being such a great helper, enjoy a special lunch with the teacher on this day:

HOW SWEET IT IS!

Because your help was so sweet,

See your teacher for a special treat!

FIRST AND IN FRONT

Step up to the front of the class and be the line leader on this day.

Hang Ten!

Enjoy ten minutes of FREE time at the computer or the center of your choice.

The Buzz Is...

Enjoy 15 minutes of FREE reading time!

Patterns

Use with " 'Berry' Good Spellers" on page 146.

I'm a "BERRY" Good Speller!

1 10 9 8 7 6 5 4 3 2

I'm a "BERRY" Good Speller!

1 10 2 9 8 3 7 6 4 5

You're One Smart Cookie!
Congratulations!

You've got all the right ingredients
to be named
Smart Cookie of the Week.
Keep up the good work!

INGREDIENTS

Awarded to: _____

Signed: _____

Date: _____

Note to the teacher: Use with "One Smart Cookie" on page 142. Before duplicating the award, write several of the ingredients your students chose on the recipe card.

Patterns

Use with "Homework Motivator" on page 148.

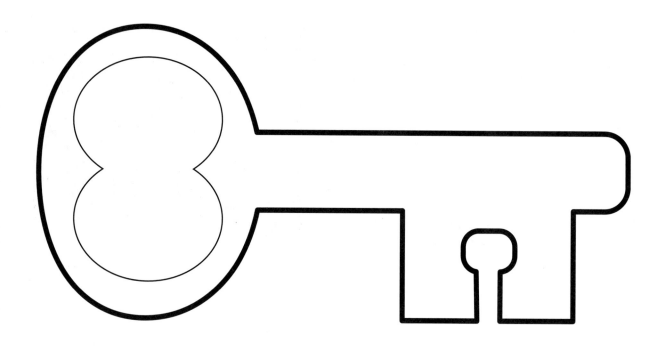

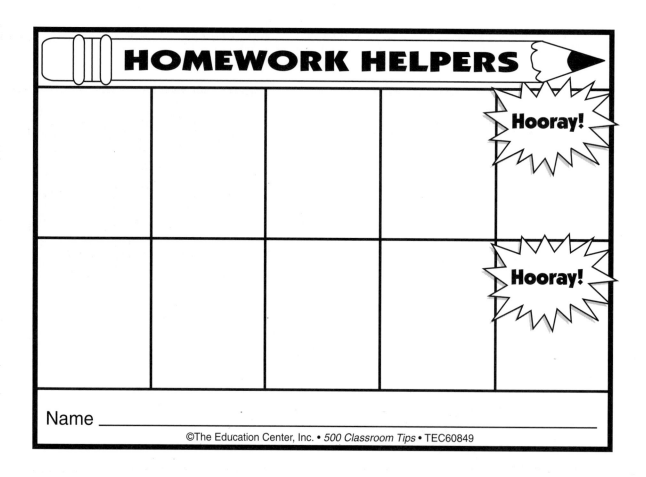

HOMEWORK HELPERS

Hooray!

Hooray!

Name _____

Patterns

Use with "HOT Tickets" and "Homework Club Card" on page 151.

Homework Club Card

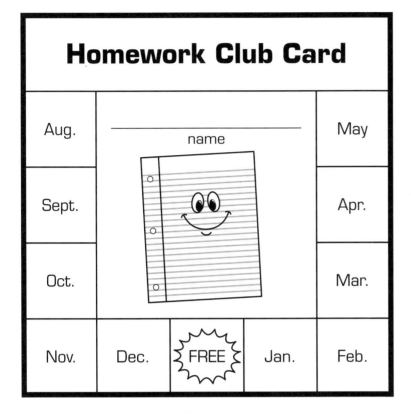

Aug.		name		May
Sept.				Apr.
Oct.				Mar.
Nov.	Dec.	FREE	Jan.	Feb.

HOT TICKET

Homework on Time

name

Homework Club Card

Aug.		name		May
Sept.				Apr.
Oct.				Mar.
Nov.	Dec.	FREE	Jan.	Feb.

HOT TICKET

Homework on Time

name

Patterns

Use with "Too Many Interruptions?" on page 157.

Is It Done Yet?

How do you know if your project is done? Use the checklist below as a guide.

Details
- [ ] Have you included all text necessary for understanding?
- [ ] Have you used illustrations to add to your project?
- [ ] Are your illustrations colorful?

Originality
- [ ] Have you written the text in your own words?
- [ ] Have you used your own creative design?

Neatness
- [ ] Is your final copy written in ink or typed?
- [ ] Have all pencil marks been completely erased?

Editing
- [ ] Are all words spelled correctly?
- [ ] Have all capitalization rules been followed?
- [ ] Have all punctuation rules been followed?
- [ ] Have you checked for correct grammar?

Comments _____

Name _____ Date _____

Is It Done Yet?

How do you know if your project is done? Use the checklist below as a guide.

Details
- [ ] Have you included all text necessary for understanding?
- [ ] Have you used illustrations to add to your project?
- [ ] Are your illustrations colorful?

Originality
- [ ] Have you written the text in your own words?
- [ ] Have you used your own creative design?

Neatness
- [ ] Is your final copy written in ink or typed?
- [ ] Have all pencil marks been completely erased?

Editing
- [ ] Are all words spelled correctly?
- [ ] Have all capitalization rules been followed?
- [ ] Have all punctuation rules been followed?
- [ ] Have you checked for correct grammar?

Comments _____

Name _____ Date _____

Note to the teacher: Use with "Is It Done Yet?" on page 157.

Check It Off!

Opening Period

Closing Period

Check It Off!

Opening Period

Closing Period

©The Education Center, Inc. • *500 Classroom Tips* • TEC60849

©The Education Center, Inc. • *500 Classroom Tips* • TEC60849

Note to the teacher: Use with "Daily Checklist" on page 160.

Communications

Contents

Class Newsletters

PHAN Mail

Increase communication between your kids and their parents with this "PHAN-tastic" idea! On Monday give each student a PHAN mail letter containing information that is **P**articularly **H**elpful **A**nd **N**ewsworthy. Include a list of homework assignments, field trip announcements, descriptions of special projects with their due dates, and other important reminders. PHAN mail will help both students and parents keep up with homework assignments and plan ahead for longer projects. It's also a great way of encouraging everyone to talk about what's happening at school.

Wendy Buehrer—Gr. 5
The Columbus Academy
Gahanna, OH

PHAN Mail
for Sept. 18–22
Homework Assignments

Monday: Use a calculator to figure out the number of seconds in a day and in a week.
Tuesday: Write definitions for igneous, metamorphic, and sedimentary rocks.
Wednesday: Write a paragraph telling why the Egyptians built pyramids.
Thursday: Study for a spelling and vocabulary test!

Reminder: Field trip Friday! Bring your lunch.

Friday-Gram

Every Friday I give a Friday-Gram to each of my students. The top portion includes a brief letter to parents describing the week's activities and important upcoming events. It also features a creative-writing sample from a different student each week. The bottom portion is an individual evaluation of the student's week at school. The evaluation includes information about the child's work habits and behavior plus space for comments. Parents sign these evaluations for students to return on Monday. I store the signed notes in each child's folder; then I refer to them during parent conferences. Parents really appreciate this weekly communication, and my students look forward to seeing their work published in the letter.

Linda Townsley—Gr. 4, Woodlands Elementary, Longwood, FL

Fifth-Grade News!

Week:

Monday

Tuesday

Wednesday

Thursday

Friday

Day-by-Day Class Newsletter

When parents ask, "What did you do in school?" arm your kids with a ready reply! At the end of each day, review with students what they learned in class. List their ideas on an overhead transparency while a student types the information on a newsletter template. At the end of the week, print copies of the completed newsletter. On the back of the newsletter, include a weekly evaluation for students to fill out with things they learned and goals they achieved. Be sure to include a space for parents to respond. If possible, also take several class photos during the week with a digital camera; then upload them into the newsletter for a firsthand view of classroom happenings. In less than ten minutes per day, you'll stay in touch with parents every week of the school year!

Fifth-Grade Team
Richmond School
St. Charles, IL

What's New?

Keep parents up-to-date with your own computerized classroom newsletter. Begin Monday by opening a new document. At the end of each day, have two to three students collaborate on a summary statement telling what happened in school that day. Have them sign the summary and save the document. Edit each day's summary. At the end of the week, print out and duplicate the resulting page to send home. Students practice real-life writing as they keep their parents informed.

Julie Eick Granchelli, Lockport, NY

On Monday: We put together our ecosystems in a bottle. We

Monday Newsletter

Put a twist on the standard Friday newsletter with this simple (and smart!) idea. Provide your students and parents with a weekly newsletter each Monday instead of at the end of the week. Use a publishing software template to create the format of the newsletter. Include sections labeled "School Happenings for the Week," "This Week's Classroom Events," "Student Birthdays," "Curriculum Activities," "Special Recognitions," and "Help Needed." With this tip, both parents and students will be fully prepared for the great week ahead!

Lori Brandman—Gr. 5, Shallowford Falls Elementary, Marietta, GA

Next Week: Field Trip!
Send a sack lunch

Friday Letter

For an easy and effective way to stay in touch, I write a Friday letter to my students' parents each week. In the letter I include events of the upcoming week, as well as any special items that students will need. Parents love this letter because it helps them plan ahead. And, if a child is not good at communicating, his parents are informed anyway!

Debbie Fly
Edgewood School
Birmingham, AL

Cool Fridge Facts!

What's the prime location in a student's home to post school news? On the fridge, of course! Every Friday afternoon, give each student a copy of page 191. Have the child list next week's vocabulary words, as well as information about upcoming tests, projects, activities, and other important events. In the notes section, instruct her to write about a goal she is working toward, a skill she is developing, or a project that's in the works. Ask each child to return her fridge facts sheet on the following Friday signed by a parent. What a cool way to keep parents in the know!

Kimberly Minafo—Gr. 4
Tooker Avenue Elementary, West Babylon, NY

Notes Home

Make contacting parents as easy as 1, 2, 3! Use a word-processing program to print each student's address and the school's return address on several self-adhesive mailing label pages. After writing a note to parents, attach the student's address label, your return address label, and a stamp to an envelope and mail. Keeping parents up-to-date is as easy as print, stamp, and send!

Michelle Trubitz—Grs. 5–6, Brookside Upper Elementary, Westwood, NJ

Learning Logs

Getting feedback from parents and informing them about your classroom is as easy as falling off a log—a learning log, that is! Each of my students has a notebook in which she writes about what she is learning in class, as well as summaries of guest speaker presentations and notices of upcoming projects. At the end of each month, I write a letter to parents about the past month and add a list of upcoming events. Each student glues a copy of this letter to a page in her log, takes her log home, and discusses it with her parents. A parent then signs the log and returns it to school. Told you it was easy!

Lea Iverson
Lincoln School
Elk River, MN

My work for the months of
_____ and _____

- I think I have improved in _____.
- My _____ needs improvement.
- In the months of _____ and _____,
  I plan to work harder on
  1. _____
  2. _____
  3. _____

Teacher's comments:

Parent's comments:

Parent's signature:

Here's How I'm Doing!

Teach students how to evaluate their work—and keep parents informed—with this easy-to-do activity. Every other month, have each student organize all of his work into a neat stack. Then provide each child with a copy of the form shown to attach to the top of his work. Direct the student to complete his part of the form, which includes areas of improvement, areas that need improvement, plus three personal goals. Goals can address specific subjects, behavior, homework, peer relations, or study skills.

On the day before students compile their work, type your comments using a computer. Then print the comments and cut them into strips. After each child finishes his work packet, have him meet with you privately to discuss your comments. Then attach the comments strip to the form. Finally, have students take their packets home to share with their parents. Parents add their comments on the form, sign it, and return it to school.

Margaret C. Cox—Grs. 1–6 Special Education
West Laboratory Elementary, Miami, FL

Evening Meeting With Parents

At the beginning of the year before open house, I meet with all parents in the evening so that those who work outside the home are able to attend. I discuss my expectations for the upcoming year and ask parents to share what expectations they have. I also provide an overview of the year. This meeting opens the lines of communication and helps parents feel more at ease when it's time for individual conferences.

Dawn Helton—Gr. 4, Read-Turrentine Elementary, Silsbee, TX

Logging Parent Contacts

Keep track of parent contacts with hassle-free ease using this simple system. First, use a computer to make a label for each student that includes her name, parents' names, and home phone number(s). Affix each label to the outside of a pocket folder. Inside the folder, keep a log of all parent contacts, as well as copies of any notes that you send home. This system eliminates lost phone number lists and makes it easy for you to document parent contacts.

Angela Wood-Hurst
Lewis and Clark Middle School
Tulsa, OK

Connie Fields
Maggie Fields   765-2868
Douglas Fields   Same

Parent-Teacher Communication

Assignment I.O.U.

Keeping track of incomplete or missing homework assignments can be a real hassle. To help me manage this paperwork problem, I developed a simple "Assignment I.O.U." form. I label an index card as shown for each student; then I place all cards in alphabetical order in a file box on my desk. When a student has an incomplete or missing assignment, she removes her card from the box and completes it with the necessary information. I check the cards several times each week so that I can make parents aware of any potential problem. Cards can easily be duplicated to send home for a parent's signature.

Sandra Preston—Gr. 5
Albany Magnet School of Humanities
Albany, NY

Assignment I.O.U.

Name: _____

Report Card Quarter: _____

Date	Assignment (subject and page #)	Reason for Incompletion	Date Completed	Teacher's Initials

Happy Face Updates

I include parents in my discipline plan from the first day of school. Every Tuesday an update folder is sent home with each student. An update sheet is stapled inside each folder (see the reproducible on page 192). Using a bright yellow marker, I give each student a happy face, a so-so face, or a sad face to denote his progress in completing assignments and classroom behavior. Student work is also sent home in this folder. Space is provided on the update sheet for the parent to write comments or ask questions. The folder is signed by the parent and returned to class the next day. This develops great parent-teacher communication.

Janice Holsteen—Gr. 5, The American School in Aberdeen, Aberdeen, Scotland

Brandon Sutton   98

1. reckoned
2. puny
3. ruefully
4. trudged
5. mite
6. popular
7. begrudged
8. nonchalantly
9. contemptuous
10. ordeal
11. sapling
12. spliced
13. gravely
14. enveous
15. diagonal

Clipped Corners

My students and their parents often wondered which assignments I recorded as grades. To solve this problem, I now make a diagonal cut across the top right-hand corner of every assignment that I record. It's easy to cut several corners at one time. Now recorded assignments are easy to spot by both students and parents.

Beth Moore—Grs. 4–5
Clark Elementary
Franklin, IN

Parent-Teacher Communication

Friday Folders

Does getting notes home to parents seem like a Herculean task? It is to some students! Help them out with this easy organizational system. Label a file folder for each child; then have her title the folder "Friday Folder" and decorate its cover with markers or crayons. Each week fill the folders with weekly progress reports, news and notes, lunch menus, and other information that parents need. Send the folders home each Friday to be signed and returned on Monday.

Maddy Smith—Grs. 3–5
St. Joseph School
Louisville, KY

Family Homework Night

Here's a terrific paper-free homework activity that involves the entire family. Designate one day a week as Family Homework Night. Give each student a two-gallon plastic storage bag filled with fun games involving problem solving and other skills. Also place a small notebook in the bag. Have students take their bags home and play the games with their parents and/or other family members; then have them write about their experiences in the notebook logs. Pain-free homework for everyone!

Marta G. Johnson—Gr. 4, Haw Creek Elementary, Asheville, NC

Comprehensive Calendar

Encourage students and their parents to plan ahead with the help of a year-at-a-glance calendar. Provide each family with a yearlong calendar at the beginning of the school year. On the calendar include dates for research papers, book reports, weekly spelling tests, field trips, science projects, special events, and standardized testing. If possible, color-code the dates to make them easy to spot.

Selena Trott
Brownell Mountain Elementary
Williston, VT

Parent-Teacher Communication

The Dog Ate It!

Accountability is key! The next time a student comes to class without his homework, have him write his reason on a sheet such as the one shown. (Duplicate these sheets on brightly colored paper so parents are sure to notice them.) Send the sheet home to inform the parent about her child's homework record. Store returned forms in a special folder to use during parent conferences.

Marcia Lehrman—Gr. 5
Maple Elementary
Indianapolis, IN

HOMEWORK NOTICE

Name: _____
Date: _____
Assignment: _____
Date due: _____
I did not bring / complete / do (circle one)
my homework because _____
_____
_____
Parent signature: _____

HOMEWORK

Testing Tip

To encourage sharing between students and parents, each test that I create totals 98 points. I instruct students to take graded tests home and share them with their parents. A student who returns his test to school signed by a parent receives two bonus points. I also provide opportunities for those students who have difficult home situations, so that they too can earn bonus points. Students are proud to share their work, and parents love not having any surprises at the end of a term.

Kathleen Jordan, Orange County Schools, Altamonte Springs, FL

You are improving!

Keep working hard!

```
✓Parent Signature Needed
  Messy: Resubmit
  Late Work Not Accepted
  Add More Detail
```

Address Labels

Keep levels of communication high and writer's cramp low by using mail-order address labels. Order labels that are printed with the phrases you write most often on students' papers. Each time you stick a label on a paper, check the phrase that's appropriate as shown. Or order labels with just two lines, each a different phrase; then cut each label in half to get two different stickers. What a simple and inexpensive way to communicate with students and parents!

Natalie S. Leatherman—Gr. 5
Pioneer Park Elementary
Lawton, OK

Parent-Teacher Communication

Up-to-the-Minute Grades

Inform parents about the status of current grades *every* time a test paper goes home with this efficient communication tip. After every test, calculate each student's current numerical grade in that subject and write it in the top right-hand corner of his test paper. Then ask that students have their parents sign and return the tests. Parents will appreciate this effort because it eliminates surprises at report card time and allows them to closely track their child's progress.

Susan E. Hollingsworth—Gr. 5
Seton Catholic School
Richmond, IN

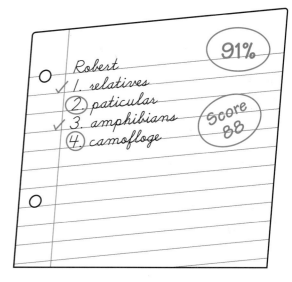

Happy Notes

Promote communication between school and home by sending positive notes to parents each quarter. Streamline this task by using blank prestamped postcards and computer-generated address labels. Print four address labels per student and affix them to the postcards; then shuffle all of the cards together and keep them on your desk as a reminder. Every other week, choose five cards and inform those students that they will receive happy notes over the weekend. Have the students decorate their cards; then write a message on each card. Mail the cards no later than Friday morning so that they'll reach their destinations over the weekend. Both parents and students will appreciate receiving positive news in the mail.

Elizabeth Brown—Gr. 4, Carlos Coon Elementary, San Antonio, TX

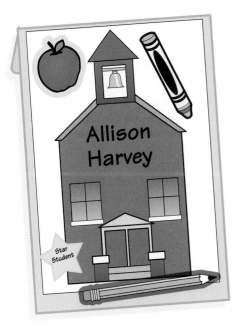

Monthly Portfolio Envelopes

Seal up a month's supply of student work with this simple idea. At the beginning of the month, provide each student with a large manila envelope and a sheet of paper from a themed or seasonal notepad. Have each student glue the sheet to the outside of her envelope; then have her decorate her envelope with drawings or stickers. Have the student keep creative work, graded tests, and photographs of special projects inside the envelope. At the end of the month, have her select the work she wants to include in her portfolio and take home the rest. Then give her a new envelope and sheet of holiday notepaper for the upcoming month. Not only does this eliminate papers stuffed in the student's desk, but it gives her the opportunity to review her work with her parents.

Joyce Hovanec—Gr. 4
Glassport Elementary
Glassport, PA

Parent-Teacher Communication

Label Reminders

Give students who need to bring or return something to school a sticky reminder! As you think of an item during the day, write it on a colorful stick-on label. Then clip the page of labels to a blank sheet kept atop the pile of papers scheduled to go home with students. At the end of the day, affix the label to that student's homework pad or planner. When the student or a parent sees the label at home, it becomes the perfect visual cue!

Jennifer Apgar
Believers' Chapel School
Cicero, NY

Return your signed math test tomorrow.

Monthly Writing Assignment

Who are the most important role models in your students' lives? Their parents! To underscore the importance of positive role-modeling, give your students' parents a brief writing assignment each month. (Stress that the assignment is optional.) Keep the finished work in each child's writing portfolio. Use the following sample topics:

- I wish I had…
- My best day in school…
- Being a parent has taught me…
- The best thing I ever did was…

Wendy Rodda—Gr. 5, Annapolis East Elementary, Middleton, Nova Scotia, Canada

Notable Notices Notebook

Create a record of the handouts you send home during the year with this simple organizational idea. Organize a three-ring binder with a divider page for each reporting period. In this binder, file a copy of each handout sent home, such as class newsletters, nine-week objectives, project instructions, and other notices. Not only will you have a record of your home communication, but you'll also have an instant portfolio at the end of the year!

Lori Huberman—Gr. 4
Centreville Elementary
Centreville, VA

Parent-Teacher Communication

Thematic Breakfasts

Many parents would love to participate in classroom activities but have work responsibilities that don't allow for school-hour visits. No problem! Once a month before the school day begins, host a thematic breakfast for parents, family members, or even the community. Post a schedule ahead of time so that parents can plan to attend. During these get-togethers, serve breakfast snacks that contribute to the theme, read books, share stories, or make art projects (see the ideas below). Parents will appreciate your extra effort to work around their busy schedules.

Theme ideas:
- Moms, Muffins, and Mysteries *(Introduce parents to great mystery books for kids.)*
- Dads, Doughnuts, and Duffel Bags *(Fill duffel bags with games, activities, and books.)*
- Pass the Poetry, Please! *(Share poetry books and student-written poetry.)*
- Breakfast for Your Brain *(Participate in activities that boost thinking skills.)*

Kimberly Minafo—Gr. 4, Tooker Avenue Elementary, West Babylon, NY

Five-Star Classroom

Increase communication with parents by turning your class into a Five-Star Classroom. Have each student bring an assignment notebook or homework folder to school. At the beginning of each day, have each child draw five stars on a dated page in his notebook. If a student is not having a good day in regard to work habits, attitude, or behavior, cross out one or more of his stars; then have him write an explanation for the parent on that page. Have students take their notebooks home nightly for parents to sign. Parents will appreciate this simple system and the communication it fosters.

Katie Kasar—Special Education Grs. 3–5, Carollton Elementary, Oak Creek, WI

Name Paolo ___

Parent Signature Requested

Great Moments in U.S. History

Answer each of the following questions in sentence form.
Refer to the timeline below to support your answers.

1. Why was the Wright Brothers' success at Kitty Hawk, North Carolina, of significance to the United States' entry into World War

Stamp Before Duplicating!

Whenever I want a particular note or reproducible activity signed by parents, I stamp a "Parent Signature Requested" message on the master copy before I duplicate it for students. With only one quick stamp, I can remind all my students to have their papers signed. Parents really appreciate this printed reminder too.

Patricia A. Walden—Gr. 5
Metter Elementary
Metter, GA

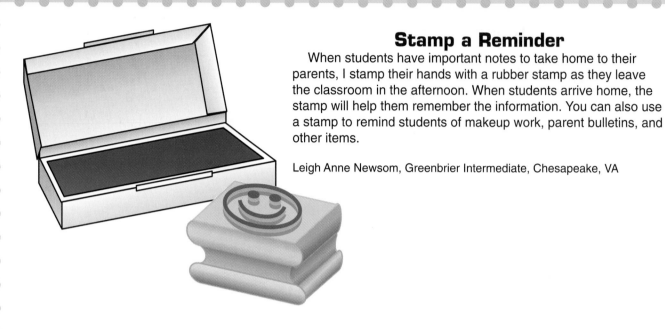

Stamp a Reminder

When students have important notes to take home to their parents, I stamp their hands with a rubber stamp as they leave the classroom in the afternoon. When students arrive home, the stamp will help them remember the information. You can also use a stamp to remind students of makeup work, parent bulletins, and other items.

Leigh Anne Newsom, Greenbrier Intermediate, Chesapeake, VA

Letters From a Teacher

Relaying all your classroom information to your students' parents can be a challenge. Gather one copy of each of the letters on your homework policy, class schedule, book clubs, and other important items; then place them in a packet titled "Letters From a [your grade level] Teacher." Send one packet home with each of your students on the first day of school. Parents will appreciate having this reference at their fingertips, and you'll feel better knowing that they've been informed.

Ann Redmond—Gr. 4, West Broad Street School, Telford, PA

Class Pizza Night

Bring your classroom family even closer together by inviting students and their families to meet at a local pizzeria once during each grading period. Several days in advance, send home a letter giving the date, time, and place to meet. If an appropriate children's movie is showing, consider taking in the film together afterward. Students and their families will love the outings, and the extra bonding that takes place will be well worth the effort!

Debbie Fly
Edgewood School
Birmingham, AL

Join the "Pizza-rific" Crowd
and Come to
Class Pizza Night

Tuesday, 6:00 P.M.
Mario's Pizza Palace
Stratford Road
Dutch Treat

Parent-Teacher Communication

Color-Coded Communicators

Combine color and clip art and what do you get? An easy way to communicate with parents! Prepare color-coded notes for parents, with each color representing a different type of message. Use clip art to add cute graphics to the notes. Then print them on half-sheets of paper. Design notes with the following messages:

- _____ had a great day today!
- I thought you'd like to know _____.
- Your child, _____, needs to make up _____.
- _____ has shown improvement in _____.
- _____ needs to improve in _____.

These notes take only a minute to complete but make a world of difference when it comes to connecting with parents!

Rebecca Amsel—Gr. 4, Yeshiva Shaarei Tzion, Lakewood, NJ

Have You Heard?

_____

had a great day today!

Ms. Amsel

has shown improvement in

Ms. Amsel

Information at Your Fingertips

Tired of spending valuable time searching for a student's phone number or address? I was, until I developed a timesaving system that gives me quick access to important student information. First, I purchased a set of ruled index cards that were attached at the top with a spiral wire. I wrote my students' names alphabetically on the cards (one child per card); then I added each child's address, phone number, and parent information on his card. I make notes directly on each card to document calls, notes home, etc. And when I need to contact parents at night, I have all the information I need in a compact, easy-to-take-home package!

Tammy L. Gilmer—Gr. 5, Orofino Elementary, Orofino, ID

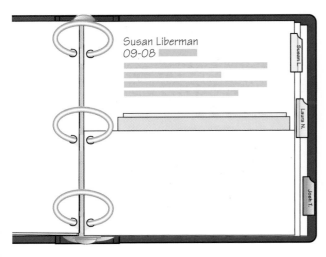

Susan Liberman
09-08

Parent-Teacher Correspondence

Keep track of parent-teacher correspondence by using pocket dividers in a three-ring binder. Label a pocket for each student. Include her birthdate and health concerns, plus her parents' names and phone number(s). In the pockets store notes to and from parents, absence excuses, conference notes, anecdotal records, copies of student work that you are concerned about, as well as anything else of importance. This easy notebook system keeps everything in one place and right at your fingertips! Use the pockets year after year by relabeling them and adding hole reinforcers.

Shirlie O. Cotoia—Grs. 3–4, Holliman Elementary, Johnston, RI

Parent-Teacher Communication

Dear Mom and Dad,

On Thursday, February 19, my class will have a math test. I will need to study pages 124–136 and do the bonus problems on pages 128, 132, and 136. I plan to study very hard.

Love,
Aimee

X *Mr. Johnson*

Keeping Parents Informed

Have students practice letter writing while they inform their parents of upcoming tests. A few days before a scheduled test, instruct each student to write a friendly letter to her parents explaining when the test will be given and what she will need to study. Direct each student to have her parent sign the letter and return it the following day. This method keeps both students and their parents informed around test time.

Martha Meadows—Gr. 5
Immaculate Heart of Mary
Cuyahoga Falls, OH

Tracking Parental Contacts

Here's a simple way to help you remember whether you've contacted a parent about a particular issue. Each time you call or send a note about a child's work on a particular assignment, highlight that score in your gradebook. One quick glance will confirm if the communication has taken place or not.

Goldie Eichorn, Yeshiva Ateres Yisroel, Brooklyn, NY

Dialing for Homework

If you've got a phone in your classroom, here's a simple idea that makes informing parents about homework assignments a breeze. Purchase an inexpensive answering machine for your class phone. At the end of each day, record the day's homework assignments on the machine. Parents and students can then call after school to make sure that all assignments have been completed. Absent students can also call to find out the work they've missed. For fun, let students take turns recording the message. Or challenge small groups of students to design flyers and business cards advertising your homework hotline to parents.

Paul Chilson—Gr. 5
East Jackson Memorial School
Jackson, MI

Tuesday's homework is...

COOL FRIDGE FACTS

for the week of _____

Student's name: _____

This week's vocabulary words:

I can...

	spell it	define it	use it in two good sentences
1. _____	_____	_____	_____
2. _____	_____	_____	_____
3. _____	_____	_____	_____
4. _____	_____	_____	_____
5. _____	_____	_____	_____
6. _____	_____	_____	_____
7. _____	_____	_____	_____
8. _____	_____	_____	_____
9. _____	_____	_____	_____
10. _____	_____	_____	_____

This week:

- We'll be working on _____ in **language arts.**
- In **math,** we will _____.
- Our current **science** unit is about _____.
- In **social studies,** we will learn about _____.
- As a class, **we are reading** the book _____
- Independently, **I am reading** _____

Important dates and notes:

_____

_____

_____

_____

Signed by: _____

Note to the teacher: See "Cool Fridge Facts!" on page 180 for information about using this reproducible.

 # Update Folder

_____ (Student)   _____ (Teacher)

| Date: | **All Work Completed** | **Behavior** |

Teacher's Comments: _____

_____

_____

Parent's Comments: _____

_____

_____

Parent's Signature _____

| Date: | **All Work Completed** | **Behavior** |

Teacher's Comments: _____

_____

_____

Parent's Comments: _____

_____

_____

Parent's Signature _____

| Date: | **All Work Completed** | **Behavior** |

Teacher's Comments: _____

_____

_____

Parent's Comments: _____

_____

_____

Parent's Signature _____

| Date: | **All Work Completed** | **Behavior** |

Teacher's Comments: _____

_____

_____

Parent's Comments: _____

_____

_____

Parent's Signature _____

Note to the teacher: Use with "Happy Face Updates" on page 182.